THE LAST PICTURE SHOW?

The Last Picture Show?

Britain's Changing Film Audience

David Docherty, David Morrison and Michael Tracey

BFI Publishing

First published in 1987 by the
British Film Institute
21 Stephen Street
London W1P 1PL

Copyright © Broadcasting Research Unit 1987

Typeset by Input Typesetting Ltd, London
Printed and bound in Great Britain by
St Edmundsbury Press,
Bury St Edmunds, Suffolk

British Library Cataloguing in Publication Data

Docherty, David
   The last picture show? : Britain's
   changing film audience.
   1. Moving-picture audiences—Great
   Britain—Statistics
   I. Title   II. Morrison, David, 1944-
   III. Tracey, Michael   IV. British Film
   Institute
   306'.485   PN1995.9.A8
   ISBN 0-85170-201-5

Contents

The research for this book was made
possible by a grant from the Leverhulme Trust.

Acknowledgements

All books rely on a large and dedicated back-up team for their production. In our case we would like to thank Anna Noble for her invaluable editorial assistance, and Kate Pluck and Shivaun Meehan for their help in typing the manuscript. Nick Moon at National Opinion Polls (NOP) and Stephen Tagg of the Social Statistics Laboratory, University of Strathclyde, provided technical expertise and support which helped to focus the research. The library staff at the British Film Institute were extremely patient with us as we rooted around looking for old books, and we thank them for that. Inspiration and advice came from many sources, and we are grateful to all those who took time to talk to us. Ian Christie and Vincent Porter, respectively Head and Acting Head of the BFI Distribution Division, were particularly helpful; furthermore, they actively promoted the idea of the RFT research, for which we thank them. The Executive Committee of the Broadcasting Research Unit were, as always, patient and helpful when discussing the research with us, and we would like to thank Brian Wenham in particular for reading and commenting on the manuscript.

The British Are Coming (Again)

THE BRITISH film industry has an unnerving habit of rushing from triumph to tragedy without pausing for breath. It is only four years since Colin Welland gave his (in)famous acceptance speech at the Oscars ceremony, when he proclaimed 'The British Are Coming'; and yet, in that time, we have had the precipitous decline of Goldcrest – the most important British film production company of the early 1980s – and the exit of Thorn EMI Screen Entertainment (TESE), whose ABC circuit comprised one third of the UK's cinemas. TESE sold out to Alan Bond (of The America's Cup fame), who, within a week, sold the company to Menachem Golan and Yoram Globus. Not long after that deal Golan and Globus' production company – Cannon – ran into major financial trouble; to survive, it sold TESE's enormous film library to United Artists, and then, even more worryingly, many of the ABC cinemas which it had acquired were sold off to property developers. To add to the industry's misery, 1986 was one of the worst years ever for film production.

One of the paradoxes of the recent history of the cinema in the UK is that the late 1970s and early 1980s was one of the most creative periods, and yet the cinema audience plummeted. By contrast 1985 and 1986 were hardly distinguished in terms of production and yet audiences increased for two consecutive years for the first time since the war: 1985 was up 18 per cent on 1984, and 1986 showed a small 3 per cent increase on 1985. This book shows why the audience behaves in such bafflingly complicated ways. It looks at when people go to the cinema, who they go with, why they go, and what they want to watch. Furthermore, as the first major study of the behaviour and attitudes of the audience for films on video, it demonstrates conclusively that video did not poach the cinema audience. It proves that cinema and video are parallel entertainments, not strict competitors. In essence the book establishes a framework for understanding the ways in which the audience for film has grown and developed since World War II.

Until 1984 it looked as if the British film industry was suffering a slow death. The first half of the 1980s showed the second highest percentage decline of any decade since the war (see Table 1), and with attendances down to 53 million in 1984 (representing just one visit to the cinema per head of population per year) it looked as if cinema exhibition had dropped below the threshold for survival. The British audience had fallen by 1986 to a figure lower than Japan, West Germany, France, Spain or Italy, not to mention the United States (see Figure 1).

Solutions aplenty were offered for reversing this decline, but what strikes the outside observer is that possible remedies

TABLE I

Quinquennial percentage decline in admissions

	%
1950–54	7
1955–59	51
1960–64	32
1965–69	34
1970–74	28
1975–79	3
1980–84	48

FIGURE I

Trends in Cinema Audiences 1960–86

Millions of Spectators

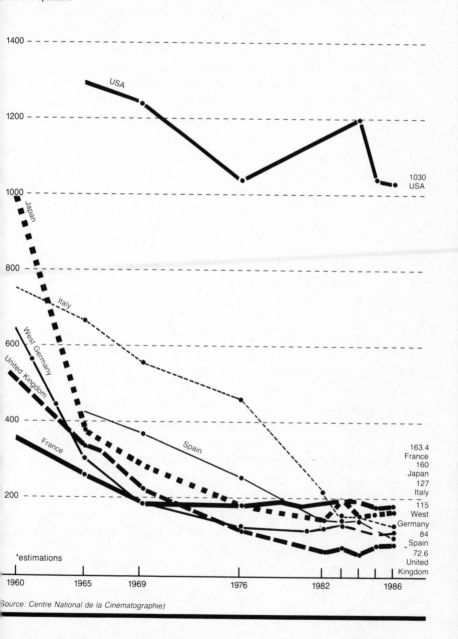

(Source: Centre National de la Cinématographie)

for the problems of the industry focused on the machinery of production and distribution. As a result of this the film industry singularly failed to grasp the social dimension of film-watching. We have to understand how films fit into people's everyday lives, as well as their family life, work patterns, leisure and culture. Only then will we fully appreciate why some people go to watch films in the cinema while most others do not, and why most film viewing takes place in the home rather than at the cinema.

The problem is that the industry refuses to come to terms with its audience as real people. Take British Film Year, for instance. This was a promotional event which began in May 1985 and ran until the Cannes Film Festival in May 1986. The campaign took the form of a roadshow exhibition with stars such as Charlton Heston, Anna Neagle and Omar Sharif and a host of lesser luminaries proclaiming the slogan: 'The cinema is the best place to watch a film'. Yet the majority of the British public disagree with this statement. According to the survey which we conducted in December 1984 (and updated in 1986), which forms the basis of this book, three-fifths of the population thought that the home was the *best* place to watch a feature film (see Table 2).

This attitude would have been inconceivable 40 years ago. In 1946 there were 1,640 million attendances at British cinemas: three-quarters of the population attended at least once a year, and one-third once a week or more. This position has now been reversed. Our survey discovered that 74 per cent of the adult population did not attend the cinema at all in 1984 (this dropped to 68 per cent in 1985), and only one in a hundred of the minority who did attend went once a week or more.

What has changed over the past forty years to bring about such a drastic decline? Why does cinema no longer play a part in the lives of most people in the United Kingdom? Down the years many stories have been told about the decline of the cinema, most focusing on the role of the television

4

TABLE 2

The best way to watch a feature film

N = 795

		Age			Class			
Weighted	Total	16–29	30–49	50+	AB	C1	C2	DE
Base	795	227	346	210	128	219	215	231
Cinema	31	39	31	21	43	38	27	20
VCR	22	31	26	6	14	20	27	24
TV	42	26	35	70	36	38	40	50
Don't know	6	4	8	4	7	4	7	6

(Due to rounding, totals do not add up 100 per cent)
(A: Upper-middle class (mostly old professions); B: middle class (lower or new professions, e.g. teachers, social workers, middle management); A1: White-collar workers; C2: Skilled working class; DE: Unskilled working class and those at lower levels of subsistence.)

set as cinema's killer. In Chapter One we demonstrate that television was framed; the real culprits were Elvis Presley, expresso coffee, the Town and Country Planning Act of 1947 and the sclerosis of the British exhibition industry. After bringing the story of the cinema audience up to date we turn to an analysis of the social structure of the audience in Chapter Two. Although the audience for cinema has been the subject of market research, a tendency remains for the reports to treat the audience as statistics wrapped in skins. There has been precious little social analysis of film use or of reasons for cinema attendance. This book contributes such an analysis. This is the first large-scale research on the audience for films on video: a portrait of this audience is drawn in Chapter Three.

The myths about the audience for film have to be examined

in the light of research which considers the role of the enter-tainment film in British life. Looking at the cinema-going public as brothers, sisters, husbands, wives, daughters, mothers, miners, clerks or lecturers will inform us about the meaning and future of film and cinema in a way that some of the more simplistic market research and subjective judge-ments never could. Finally, in the midst of the social analysis of the causes of, and reasons for, cinema attendance and video viewing we have not ignored the vital question of taste. In Chapter Four we outline the relationship between film taste and people's social experience. We explode old myths about the relationship between film and working-class culture by presenting a fresh look at some hoary old ques-tions: we actually asked people what they like, and why they like it.

In the past the denizens of Wardour Street, where the decisions about the cinema are made, have been happy to rely on their own myths about the audience, built up over the years of 'touch it, feel it' judgements. Consequently there has been a tendency to resist audience research. In his over-view of film audience research, Bruce Austin argues that there has been 'little in the way of systematic, reliable, and theoretically-grounded research . . . focused on the recipients or consumers of theatrically exhibited pictures.' (Austin 1983: xvii) With one or two exceptions (in particular Tudor 1974) most film research in Britain has focused on the cinema as an economic or industrial process, or on films as quasi-texts, analysed in the same way that one would a novel or a dream. The people at the heart of the system – the audience – have been somewhat ignored. There are many reasons for this, not least the reluctance of the film industry to divulge its own market research, or sponsor independent academic research. Furthermore, although there have been literally hundreds of American studies on different aspects of the audience (see Austin 1983) little theoretical advance has been made. Academic audience research is split broadly into psychological and sociological camps; each has its own theoretical baggage, research concerns and methods, and, possibly as a result of concentrating on one aspect of the filmic experience, neither is particularly well developed. We will take each in turn, highlighting the failings of particular approaches, but demonstrating how they raise questions which we have addressed in our research.

Attitudes and Actions: The Sociology of Film

Because the research base for the sociology of film is extremely limited, most theoretical work is based on abstract armchair speculation. Sociologists and communications researchers have consistently related the great sociological themes to the cinema. Some neo-Marxists, like Adorno, have argued that Hollywood films express the progressive alienation of the individual. (Andrae 1979) Others researchers, including the United States Information Agency (1965), suggest that the spread of American culture and ideology is facilitated by Hollywood. There is a great deal of somewhat confused discussion of the central question: do films *reflect* values, ideologies, norms, etc. or are these *created* by films? Unfortunately, since many of the studies cited in the theoretical literature are based on limited research with students rather than with the general population we have no definitive answers to this question.

Recent research has focused on the relationship between film taste and general attitudes to the cinema. (Austin 1982; Robinson 1984) In our thinking on the subject we were influenced by an idea from Ian Jarvie. He tried to escape the sterile and unhelpful discussion about films and values by focusing on the ways in which films act as problem-solving devices which allow adolescents to play out moral and cultural dilemmas in their imaginations. (Jarvie 1982) In Chapter Four we extend this and look at the ways in which

7

films are involved in a complex negotiation of the relationship between the everyday world and the world of pleasure.

As well as the great questions of value and culture, sociologists have traditionally been interested in the reasons people give for attending the cinema or a particular film. For instance, Elihu Katz and Paul Lazarsfeld developed the theory of the two-step flow, which argued that ideas pass from the media to opinion leaders, who inform the rest of the population. 'Movie-going . . . is not a solitary activity', they suggested. 'People go to the movies in groups. The flow of influence in this realm, we think, takes place largely within these movie-going groups, which are usually made up of age peers. But when it comes to consulting a movie "expert", people of all ages turn to the girls.' (1955: 308) Following in this tradition we asked a range of questions concerning the social relationships involved in the decision to attend the cinema or hire a video: who people went to the cinema with turned out to be a crucial clue in reconstructing the reasons why they attended at all.

Some sociologists, given to flights of fancy, have developed a kind of social speculation, looking at disaster or science fiction movies as reflections of tensions about technology or as representing a desire to escape from present political realities into a new frontier (for example Kelly 1979, Gans 1978, Elliott and Schenck-Hamling 1979). Although a nice way to spend an afternoon, this work is little more than a sociological parlour game. It has no research base to speak of, and it had no influence on our research. Speculation is valuable, for without it we would not be able to develop imaginative and insightful hypotheses, but if speculative propositions are not tested against actual audience behaviour and attitudes, they are a waste of time. Above all else the sociology of film requires the kind of research base which this book provides.

The Pleasure Principle: The Psychology of Film

Psychologists of every shade and variety have theories about audience reactions to films. Empirical psychologists have worried away at the effects of films on behaviour since the 1920s and early 1930s, when the Payne Foundation Studies explored the supposedly pernicious effects of films on children and adolescents (see Young 1935). Although there was some controversy surrounding their findings – and their sponsors rewrote the research to make films appear dangerous – the unsurprising conclusion of the research was that behaviour was conditioned by family life, environmental setting and individual psychic propensities. Films were held to make only a short-term, relatively marginal contribution to psychopathic or sociopathic conditions.

Although the Payne researchers spent the best part of a decade on the project, the issues were not resolved. Psychologists continued to work on the problem, pressurised by the moral and intellectual establishment, which believed that films must do some harm if people enjoyed them. In 1936 the appropriately named Most Reverend John J. Cantwell wrote, 'So great is the power of the motion picture to impress the youth of the land that one hour spent in the darkness of the cinema palace, intent on the unfolding of the wrong kind of story, can and frequently does nullify years of careful training on the part of the Church, the school, the home.' The great man blamed this on the fact that 75 per cent of Hollywood writers were 'pagans . . . who care nothing for decency, good taste and refinement.' He went on to say: 'Most of them are living lives of infidelity and worse, wherein there is to be found not a suggestion of respect for religion or for spiritual values.' (1936: 13–25)

Psychologists were also interested in the relationship between morally ambiguous audio-visual stories and the behaviour of those continuously exposed to this material. One of the Payne Foundation researchers, J. G. Cressey, summed up his theoretical position in a 1938 article which argued that the experience of film was modified by background and personality and he presented a holistic understanding of the audience. 'Going to the movies', he argued, 'is a unified experience involving always a specific film, a specific personality, a specific social situation and specific time and mood.' (1938: 517)

He distinguished three psychological states which film viewers enter into: first, some members of the audience project onto the actor or role characteristics which they themselves possess; second, others in the audience incorporate or introject some aspects of the film's world into their own attitudes and self-perception; third, some audience members will identify with the world of the film and accept certain values as a result of the film, whilst retaining a full awareness of themselves and their own values. Cressey argued that each of these states was the result of a range of background factors, and therefore 'cinema should not be conceived as a unilateral social force, but as a reciprocal relationship of screen and spectator, of screen patterns and values, and of social patterns and social values.'

Cressey's rather sensible and moderate argument has often been ignored in favour of scaremongering about violence and sex on the one hand, and class analysis of cinema as an opiate of the masses on the other. Furthermore, each variety of psychoanalysis has a version of the cinema-dream machine theory. Early versions of what Augst calls 'the lure of psychoanalysis in film theory' (1980: 415) were articulated by film critics. Kracaeur argued that film audiences 'crave to be released from the grip of consciousness', and therefore when they go to films they are no longer themselves but take on the roles projected by the film. (1960: 599) Parker Tyler wrote: 'Hollywood is but the industrialisation of the mechanical worker's dream ... extended ritualistically into those hours reserved by custom for relaxation and amusement.' He went on to note 'the tendencies of screen stories to emphasise – unintentionally – neuroses and psychopathic traits discovered and fomulated by psychoanalysis.' (Greenberg 1976: 9–10)

Conventional Freudian interpretations tended to suggest that films throw up some unwanted and unconscious wish, and then explain the wish away, giving the audience the simultaneous pleasure of the unconscious appearing and then being safely dealt with. Harvey Greenberg's book, *The Movies on Your Mind*, follows in this tradition: 'At the cinema', he argues, 'consciousness is . . . lulled. Vision is directed within, then drawn outward again to the screen; and mind coils subtly between the seductive images; personal and cinematic fantasy interpenetrate. Past conflicts are processed – but never in the psychoanalytic sense, for conscious insight is not the intention. Instead, our deepest terrors and longings are mimed, simultaneously expressed whilst they are denied.' (ibid: 8)

In the late 1960s and early 1970s film theory turned again to psychoanalysis, searching for theoretical models of greater sophistication which would produce a better understanding of the relationship between the spectator and the film. The initial effect of the structuralist intervention into film theory was to take the audience for granted; the proper interest for those analysing films was held to be the film itself (or the text, as the new film theory called it). (Eckert 1973) The meaning of the 'text' was constituted by its internal structures, and the spectator simply worked as decoder, much like the receiver of a message in morse code. Though the spectator might misinterpret the meaning, or the wires might be cut and the message not come across, spectators could not add to the meaning of what was encoded. But disenchantment set in with this model; it was difficult to ignore the multiplicities of different meanings which theorists and the public extracted from films. Furthermore, if films were self-contained the critic had to adopt a passive role in the creation of film culture, a position which few critics wished to accept. As a result many decided that the spectator was, after all, an active participant in the interpretation of a film. (Casetti 1984)

Rewriting Freud, as refracted through the work of the French psychoanalyst Jacques Lacan, the film theorist Christian Metz argued that the spectator did indeed make an active interpretive contribution, in that he or she had to negotiate constantly between accepting the film as real and yet knowing it to be an invention. Such a position for the spectator could be shown to be related to certain stages in the development of consciousness according to the Freudian schema. (Metz 1975)

The problem with such informulations is that however ingenious and indeed insightful they may be, they tell us very little about the multiplicity of ways in which films are actually interpreted or audio-visual works experienced. Psychoanalysis often poses interesting questions, but its answers often lack explanatory power in the context of real people in actual, often widely varying, situations.

In the late 1970s John Ellis tried to reconcile research on the empirical viewer and on the theoretical spectator (Ellis 1978), and a little later Casetti wrote of the need to reconcile 'the requirement of a flesh and blood individual and the elaboration of a symbolic construction'. (1984: 27) It is the former who is the subject of this book: someone who has a job, or is unemployed; is a father, mother, daughter, brother; is fourteen and worrying about spots; eighteen and worried about the bomb; thirty and worried about the family; a feminist, a conservative or apolitical; in short, a living, breathing person.

In the research for this book we tried on many occasions to reconcile both positions, to find a way to understand the spectator theoretically, as the point of intersection of various signifying systems and institutional determinants, at the same time as finding out about how real live individuals experience the cinema. Whilst we do not believe that the attempt is fruitless, we have been unable to bring the two together. As a result, our book is concerned with what we have been able to establish empirically about actual audience behaviour and attitudes. We believe that as such it is more than just a contribution to the debate about the audience. It is the *only* properly funded piece of social research on the nature of the film audience in contemporary Britain.

CHAPTER 1

Living in a Material World:
The Cinema Audience 1946–86

EACH MYTH has its Golden Age when heroes walked the earth. The age is invariably betrayed by negligence or evil, which break the bond between mankind and its natural state. The ways in which the decline in British cinema is understood conform to this mythologising process. The Golden Age of the cinema is related to a view of the Golden Age of British public life. This time may be known as BT (Before Television). During this Golden Age the working class lived and worked in integrated communities, the families who played together stayed together, and cinemas were pleasure domes where the British could live out their fantasies. The great British heroes of this age were James Mason and Margaret Lockwood (who topped the *Daily Mail*'s National Film Awards – which had over two million voters – as well as the Bernstein Questionnaires run by the Granada group); Anna Neagle and Michael Wilding, who starred in the top film of 1947, *Piccadilly Incident* and 1949's award-winner *Spring in Park Lane*; and others such as Stewart Granger, Ann Todd and John Mills.

On the surface nothing much changed during the next ten years. The top film of 1956 was *Reach for the Sky*, with Kenneth More playing the British war hero Douglas Bader, and although new stars such as Dirk Bogarde and Diana Dors emerged they were essentially little different from their predecessors. These apparent continuities are undermined by the inescapable fact that during the ten years which separated

Piccadilly Incident and *Reach for the Sky* the annual cinema audience dropped from 1,640 to 1,101 million: a loss of 500 million. This process continued, and by 1960 when Dirk Bogarde achieved top box-office status for the second time with *Doctor in Love* (which was closely followed at the box office by *Carry on Constable*) the audience had plummetted by another 600 million to 501 million.

The Golden Age was well and truly over. Betrayed, many felt, by the negligence of the owners of the cinema chains and by the evil of television. This interpretation of history has led to two prevailing myths concerning the decline of the cinema in Britain, each of which has had a profound effect on the survival strategies adopted by successive governments and by the industry itself. The myth of the universal audience states that once upon a time everyone went to the cinema and that the way forward for the cinema is an indiscriminate attempt to lure them back. The myth of technological evolution states that cinema has been fighting a losing battle against the tide of technological development, so that cinema has inevitably had to give way to television as part of the march of history.

Examined in the light of historical and sociological evidence these myths end up looking slightly threadbare, like the hand-me-down stories of a fading empire. There were three distinct phases of decline in the audience: from 1946 to 1954 the audience fell by around 9 per cent; there was a 51 per cent drop between 1955 and 1959; and since 1960 (apart from the disasters of 1981 and 1984 and the small recovery in 1985 and 1986) there has been a slow continuous fading away of the audience. This decline is not a uniquely British phenomenon, indeed it is common to the developed world (see Figure 1). But there are particular elements in the British case which are peculiar to this country, and by examining the three phases of the decline we will throw light on the processes underlying the changes in the audience.

1 Losing the Peace: 1946–54

Let us begin with the moment of glory. In 1946 more than four-fifths of the population went to the cinema at least once during the year. Not only did the bulk of the public go to the cinema, a substantial portion went several times a week (see Table 3, also Abrams 1949, Moss and Box 1943, Hulton Research 1947, England 1950). Although the myth of the universal audience is apparently substantiated by these figures, a bit of digging shows that those who did not attend regularly were as important to the future of the cinema as those who did.

TABLE 3

Frequency of cinema visits 1949

N = 13,000

Age	16–24	23–34	35–44	45+
	%	%	%	%
Twice a week	40	18	1	9
Once a week	32	32	25	17
Once or twice a month	15	19	17	14
Few times a year	10	22	30	32
Never	3	9	14	28
Total	100	100	100	100

Class	Upper	Middle	Lower
	%	%	%
Twice a week	8	13	19
Once a week	20	24	24
Once or twice a month	23	18	14
Few times a year	34	31	24
Never	15	14	19
Total	100	100	100

(Upper = top 14%   Middle = next 20%   Lower = 66%)
(*Source: Hulton Research 1949*)

Almost half of the population over 35 did not attend the cinema, or attended very infrequently. This was also true of upper- and middle-income groups. By comparison half of the cinema tickets sold in any given week were bought by the young, urban working class. This was confirmed by a Gallup survey in 1948 (see Table 4).

TABLE 4

'Have you been to the cinema in the past three weeks?'

	Yes	No
	%	%
Total	57	43
Men	55	45
Women	59	41
Ages:		
18–20	79	21
21–29	76	24
30–49	57	43
50–64	45	55
65+	34	66

(Source: Gallup)

Age, education, income and class combined to produce a film audience which was primarily young and working-class (both industrial and white-collar). By and large although a significant proportion of the rest of the population attended the cinema they did not do so regularly or with the same commitment. Whilst it was quite common for young people to see around two hundred films in a year, their parents and grandparents were likely to see a handful, if any at all. The dictates and rhythms of family life created the conditions for cinema attendance. In general the pattern was that a young couple would attend the cinema very regularly whilst courting; after marriage, the first years of setting up home and having children drained the energy, and resources and cinema-attendance dropped off. It picked up again for a short period while the children were growing up and the parents had to do something with them. This second stage normally took the couple into their mid-30s, by which time their interest in cinema and out-of-home leisure was considerably reduced. As we shall see in the next chapter this pattern has not changed since the 1940s.

TABLE 5

Attendance by marriage and children: 1948

	Never Go/Very Seldom
	%
Married	39
Single	28
Married Women:	
No Children	40
Children 0–4	44
Children 5–15 years	30

(Source: Gallup)

One of the curiosities of the decline in the audience in the 1950s was that this audience was drawn from the generation which had been the most committed to cinema as adolescents and children. Their quite extraordinary level of engagement and involvement with the cinema in the 1940s did not carry into their lives as adults and teenagers in the 1950s.

One reason for the increase in attendance of children and adolescents in the 1940s was the rise of the cinema club (see Table 7).

TABLE 6

Percentage attendance at the cinema of children under 16 in 1948 and 1931

N = 21,000 (1931) = 14,500 (1948)

	At least twice a week		Once a week		Sometimes, not regular		Never	
	1948	1931	1948	1931	1948	1931	1948	1931
Age	%	%	%	%	%	%	%	%
15–16	22	*	41	*	36	*	1	*
11–14	31	11	38	30	29	53	2	6
8–10	31	9	41	32	24	51	4	8
5–7	14	8	32	29	36	41	18	22
3–4**	5	7	12	23	43	33	40	37

* 15–16 year-olds were not included in the 1931 survey.

** In 1948 most of the under-fives polled were 4 years old.

(Source: Hughes (London County Council) 1951)

TABLE 7

Membership of cinema clubs in London: 1948

Age group	15–16	11–14	8–10	5–7
Percentage of members	30%	33%	50%	22%

Source: Hughes (London County Council) 1951

These clubs, which were run partly by committees of children, tied the cinema to every aspect of a child's life. 80 per cent of members attended regularly and the clubs ran competitions in drawing, painting, essay-writing, model aeroplane building, solo singing, instrumental playing, tap dancing. There were football teams that played against other cinema clubs, Saturday rambles, swimming and table tennis. Some clubs, in collaboration with the police, gave instructions in road safety; one club arranged an educational visit to County Hall. Many clubs even sent out birthday cards to their members. On top of this there were club songs and club promises such as 'I promise to tell the truth, to help mother, and try to make this great country of ours a better place to live in.' (Hughes 1951: 10) Despite this attempt to keep up standards of orderliness, with monitors for blocks of seats, and prizes for good behaviour, the clubs were bedlam on Saturday mornings. The older groups often complained that that they could not enjoy the cinema because of disorder, whistling, booing and tumultuous cheering by the younger children.

Levels of education had a great deal to do with levels of cinema attendance. The average attendance of a pupil at a secondary modern school in 1948 was 1.8 times a week whilst the average of grammar school pupils was only 0.9 times a week. This difference was not simply the result of homework or cost, as can be seen from the fact that 80 per cent of secondary modern pupils wanted to go twice a week to the cinema compared to less than 50 per cent of grammar school pupils (Dodman 1948). The crux of the difference lay in leisure options and home conditions.

Dodman reported that many respondents gave the size of family and overcrowding at home as a reason for cinema attendance; people simply wanted 'a little peace and quiet'. But there was more to it than that. The extended family and friendship networks of working-class communities made the cinema a central component in popular public culture, whereas the home conditions of grammar school children were considerably better, and when they did go out they had a broader range of leisure options available to them.

A remarkable series of letters sent to the sociologist J. P. Mayer in 1945 bears out the importance of the family network. According to one correspondent: 'As a child, I went to the pictures with my family; father, mother and younger brother. As far as I remember we went about once a month, whenever there was something good on. . . . At ten I began going regularly once a week with a girl friend.' (Mayer 1946: 19)

This pattern was confirmed by other letters: 'My first introduction to films was at the age of seven; when my parents, who had been taking turns at going out, decided that I was big enough to go with them they took me about once a fortnight to one of the local cinemas.' (ibid: 53) 'My interest in films was first awakened when I was expected to accompany my elder brothers and sisters to the nearest cinema perched on a hill some two miles distant, so that my parents were free to choose their particular choice of entertainment on Saturday afternoons.' 'My first contact with the screen was when I went, together with my elder sisters, to the "Mickey Mouse Club".' (ibid: 62) 'I used to go with my three cousins and our grandmother, and we sat in the back row of the cheapest seats, which cost only fourpence. . . . When I was twelve our numbers had decreased from four to three. My eldest cousin started working at the local printers, and was therefore too important to go with us to the cinema.' (ibid: 65) 'My parents being somewhat narrow-minded didn't approve of me going to the movies so young, but my youngest aunt rescued me from a somewhat restricted future and often called for me, with the intention of taking me to see a movie.' (ibid: 80)

The importance of the extended family in stimulating cinema attendance can be seen from the next quotation: 'My grandmother, an ardent film serial fan, went to the pictures on every pension evening (Friday). She enjoyed taking me and my young cousin for company. The three of us became well-known to the commissionaire, box office girl and the usherettes. . . . When I was moved away from my grandmother, it meant no more films for me. No more, in fact, for three years. Oddly enough, it did not bother me. . . . [Eventually] I went regularly, sometimes twice a week with the boy-friends. That was because I preferred sitting in a cinema than strolling the streets.' (ibid: 62)

Clearly the family and the close local community were important in the formation of leisure habits, so much so that if these conditions changed then regular cinema attenders became irregular or non-attenders. In the 1940s habitual cinema-going was a social experience rather than the product or expression of a deep-seated psychological or cultural need. But although leisure habits formed cinema attendance, there can be little doubt that films had a profound influence on the regular audience. One correspondent wrote: 'films have undoubtedly influenced me . . . because I always talk to myself in an American accent, and often think that way too. Most of the films I have seen were American because American films are the best.' (ibid: 20)

The American influence led many of the young correspondents into *Billy Liar* territory. As the next series of quotations shows, many became dissatisfied with the drabness and austerity of post-war Britain: 'When I've been to see a film (especially one in Technicolor) I always walk home feeling disgusted with the drab town I live in, the paint-work of the doors, etc. seems awfully dull and dresses look plain after seeing the glorious scenery and the stylish clothes in the film'; (ibid: 42) 'films make me look down upon neighbours and I think them ugly, fat and ignorant. I go to school in the country and despise country people'; (ibid: 49) films make me 'dissatisfied with my present existence'. (ibid: 51).

Although the reasons for attending the cinema were social rather than psychological, the social reasons produced fertile conditions for a profound engagement with films. Regular attendance at the cinema meant that, more than any generation before or since, the young regular audience in the late 1940s was highly committed to the cinema and profoundly influenced by the films. So what went wrong?

2 The Death of a God: 1955–60

In an impassioned letter one of Mayer's correspondents wrote, 'The screen is to me a God.' (ibid: 53) One morning Britain woke up to find that God was dead, or rather that monotheism had given way to polytheism. New gods such as washing machines, fridges, cars, record players, and televisions were being worshipped, and the cinema was demoted in the Pantheon. One feature of myths is that when disaster occurs a myth looks to an objective external force as the cause. Interpreters of the great cinema disaster did not look to a malevolent demiurge as the reason for the decline but they did fall back on the great movement of history. The presiding spirit of this movement was television.

During the 1950s television appeared to be the obvious enemy. Most researchers and commentators focused on the television/cinema connection. There were good reasons for this in that to all intents and purposes television inhabited the same terrain as the cinema. It was visual; it was entertainment-based; and it was expanding as cinema was declining.

There was an increase in television licences from 343,000 in 1950 to 10 million in 1960. At the same time cinema audiences declined from 1,396 million in 1950 to 515 million in 1960. There seemed to be no reason therefore to search for another explanation for the decline in attendances. The answer was straightforward: the audience was simply staying at home to watch the telly.

Two different calculations need to be examined if the influence of television is to be properly evaluated. First, the ratio of cinema closure to attendance in the early 1950s reveals that every time a cinema closed 75 per cent of the attendances at that cinema were lost. (Spraos 1962: 37) In other words, the location of the cinema in the local neighbourhood was vital in the formation and maintenance of the cinema-going habit.

On the other hand, the ratio of television licences issued

to cinema closures shows that television was not the only reason for the decline. A government report in 1958 showed that for every television licence taken out between 1950 and 1954 a loss of around 65 cinema admissions occurred. (PEP: 1958) According to this calculation the 1958 figure of 9 million licences should have equalled 585 million fewer admissions but by 1958 attendances had in fact dropped by 900 million from their 1946 high of 1,640 million. Only two-thirds of the decline would be attributable to television licences according to this calculation of the 1950–4 trend.

The loss of 65 admissions for each television licence is in fact too high. It would mean that for every new licence taken out two regular cinema-attenders stopped going altogether. This is highly unlikely because, as the figures for the audience in the 1940s demonstrated, the bulk of the audience was young and working-class, a group who did not have access to television in a major way until the late 1950s. Furthermore, even when they did have access to television, the leisure habits of single people below the age of 24 would have militated against them becoming heavy television viewers.

Even the introduction of commercial television with its emphasis on entertainment did not have quite the effect which has been attributed to it. For there to have been a decrease in the number of cinema attendances the average hours of viewing would have had to increase. Such an increase did not take place. A survey conducted in the town of Reading in 1958 showed that, of those with commercial television 7 per cent attended the cinema twice a week. This was only 2 per cent less than those without a television at all. Of those who did not go to the cinema at all, there was only a 4 per cent difference between those with commercial television and those without a television. One final point on the statistics of decline: the number of television licences roughly stabilized among cinema-going groups in the early 1960s; after that point older or more affluent people bought televisions, but as they were not regular cinema-goers these licences would not have affected the figures; and yet attendances continued to decline apace.

Rather than asserting a causal connection between cinema and television it is more accurate to say that the rise in television was caused by the *same* process underlying the decline in cinema attendance. Just as the conditions for the cinema emerged during one phase of industrial capitalism, which created a working class concentrated in large industrial conglomerations, with increased leisure time and a financial surplus; so the conditions for television were created by the rise in real wages, comfortable homes and the emergence of the nuclear family, which was concurrent with the sense that the working-class extended family was breaking up.

The development of a consumer culture, with its emphasis on consumer durables and its focus on the home, squeezed the amount of leisure surplus available, and shifted the emphasis of that expenditure. Between 1946 and 1958 incomes rose at a higher rate than did the cost of living. Most of this increase in incomes was spent on consumer goods. In 1958 one home in two had a vacuum cleaner as opposed to one in seven in 1939; one in five had a washing machine as opposed to one in fifty in 1939; one home in fifteen had a refrigerator as against one in fifty in 1939; the number of motor cars increased from 1.9 million in 1939 to 4.2 million in 1958. In this process cinema was squeezed out.

The Town and Country Planning Act of 1947 completely transformed the conditions for a successful cinema industry. The Act led to the clearing of slums, the growth of new towns, the rebuilding of city centres and, crucially, the re-siting of large sections of the working class. Between 1931 and the 1970s the inner cities lost around one-third of their population while the number of people living around the edges of the cities grew by around one-quarter. (Lawless and Brown 1986) The population which sustained the cinema in the inner cities moved out. Another important factor was the rise in owner-occupation. In 1947 only one-quarter of the population of England and Wales owned their own homes; by 1972 the proportion had grown to over half of the population. (Elliott B 1984: 32) The extension of owner-occupation led to better, more spacious and comfortable housing and a greater psychological commitment to the home. (see Table 8).

TABLE 8

Cinema-going analysed by home ownership: 1958

	Own Home	Rent Un-furnished	Rent Furnished	Living with Parents	Resi-dential	Total
	%	%	%	%	%	%
Once a week	7	11	28	38	35	17
Once a month	15	18	35	31	31	21
6 times a year	15	13	12	17	14	14
3 times a year	18	15	8	6	10	14
Not in last year	45	43	17	8	11	34

(Source: PEP 1958)
* Residential means people living in publicly administered homes, lodging houses, etc.

Apart from changes in the ecology of the city the cinema audience was affected by a cultural revolution – the emergence of the teenager. When working-class teenagers were simply 'young adults', without a distinctive culture or a wide range of leisure pursuits, cinema fitted easily into their lives; but the symbolism of teenagers ripping up cinema seats when Bill Haley played *Rock Around the Clock* was pregnant with meaning. This was one of those crucial points which marks the beginning of a new culture. Cinema could not withstand the onslaught of Rock and Roll, Trad Jazz, espresso (Bongo or otherwise), motorbikes, duffle coats and leather jackets, the Bomb, and the panoply of artefacts and opinions which made up youth culture from the mid-1950s. Although the young working class did not completely stop going to the cinema in this period – indeed proportionately they represented more of the audience – they stopped going as regularly as they had (see Table 9). The simplest explanation is that they had other things to do, but clearly at a deeper level a cultural transformation set in which left cinema struggling in its wake.

TABLE 9

'How often do you go to the cinema nowadays?' (1958)

N = 1000

	%
Twice a week	7
Once a week	15
Once a fortnight	5
Once a month	8
Less than once a month	36
Never	29
	100

This survey was conducted in Reading and may therefore have some limitations if applied to the country as a whole, but, as we saw with figures culled from it in the discussion of the effect of commercial television, several important points can be made on the basis of it. First, those who attended the cinema once a week or more were down from 36 per cent in 1948 to 22 per cent in 1958. Equally important is the rise in the number who went less than once a month:

in 1948 this was around 24 per cent of the population but by 1958 the number had grown to 36 per cent. Even the mainstays of the industry – the 16–24 age group – did not go as regularly; in 1958 around half of them attended once a week or more, as opposed to around four-fifths in 1948. Finally, and interestingly, the number who no longer went at all rose by only 9 per cent, from 20 per cent to 29 per cent. It is clear that the great decline in attendances was like the slow unwinding of a clock spring.

In spite of social, psychological and cultural changes the decline in the audience need not have been quite as extensive. Certainly there is no doubt that with an increased number of leisure options the cinema would inevitably have suffered, but it might have settled at around a quarter of its 'natural' pre- and post-war figure of 900–1,000 million.

The film industry believed that its fight was with a new alternative technology for delivering moving pictures. Instead of re-siting the cinemas and following the audience to the new housing estates, therefore, the film industry struck back at the technological level. It attempted to combat the smallness of the television screen by utilising techniques which emphasised the largeness of the cinema screen. CinemaScope, Cinerama, 3-D and a greater emphasis on Technicolor were wheeled out, so that the viewer would recognise that a 10-inch black and white screen, which showed only one channel (ITV was not generally available until 1957 at least), was an inferior form of visual entertainment.

This view, understanding the decline of the cinema as the result of technology, led either to great pessimism about technological evolution ('television will inevitably prevail over the cinema') or great optimism based on the poor technical quality of the television screen. In mythic terms the Calvinists believed that cinema was doubly predestined to death whereas television had the marks of grace, and the Arians believed that if you preached well enough, long enough and widely enough people would flock back to their first God. Either way these mythic interpretations ignored the realities of the great social changes that were occurring outside the cinema, and fundamentally misunderstood the relationship between the audience for television and the audience for the cinema.

3 The Long Goodbye: 1961–86

After the great decline came the slow death. Between 1961 and 1984 audiences declined from 515 million to 54 million. Each year was greeted with optimism that the new films would turn the decline around, and each year ended with the conclusion that they did not make films like they used to. The great financial disasters of *Cleopatra*, *Doctor Doolittle*, and *Hello Dolly*, which were indiscriminately aimed at the general audience, caused much heart-searching in Hollywood, particularly when Peter Fonda made *Easy Rider* for chewing gum and buttons only to see it become one of the top grossing films of the year. Either way, the films had no effect on general audience levels. No matter whether it was thrills, spills, sex, violence, Sensurround, Smellaround, Cinerama, 3-D, Dolby B, Dolby C, 70 mm, the audience stubbonly refused to increase their attendance habits.

Surveys from this period show that the structural changes of the 1950s had undermined the cinema to such an extent that stabilization, let alone growth, was no longer possible. The number who had stopped going completely remained around the 40 per cent mark throughout the 1960s, but regularity of attendance continued to decline. Indeed, by 1970 only 2 per cent of the population went to the cinema once a week or more, compared to one-third of the population in the late 1940s (the twice a week category became virtually obsolete as means of classifying attendances at this point). The bulk of those who attended the cinema went less than five times a year.

By 1970 the cinema had become just one more leisure pursuit among a myriad of alternatives. It had very little pulling power of its own, and structural conditions (such as housing and work) were no longer conducive to such mass participation pursuits. The cinema had to fight for its place in the sun, but a vicious downward spiral set in whereby the continued decline in the audience led to lack of confidence in the market and therefore to a lack of investment in new cinema buildings. This in turn led to increasing audience complaints about the comfort and quality of many remaining cinema buildings and to a further unwinding of attendance levels.

Furthermore, because the American audience too had declined drastically the Hollywood machine no longer pumped out films to the same degree. This meant that independent exhibitors struggled to find material and the small, poorly equipped cinemas rapidly went out of business. This led in turn to further falls in attendance. One of the ironies was that the generation who were frequent cinema attenders in the late 1940s in all probability went to the same building regularly in the 1960s and 1970s, but by then the cinema building had become a bingo-hall.

Apart from a small upward blip in the figures around the time of *Star Wars* the audience continued its slow fade away until the 1979–84 recession. The attendant unemployment struck at the heart of the audience, which declined from 120 million in 1979 to 54 million in 1984 (although it had picked up to around 70 million by 1986). The crucial aspect of the recession was that for the first time the class base of the cinema was completely transformed. Unemployment rose from 855,000 in 1975 to between three and a half and four million in 1984. In some parts of the country youth unemployment rose to over 50 per cent, and 650,000 of those officially in employment were in very low paid government-sponsored schemes. Under these circumstances it is hardly surprising that cinema has in many ways gone up-market, becoming, to a degree never before seen, a lower middle-class leisure pursuit.

TABLE 10

Decline in attendance by class: 1977–83

	Never	Infrequent	Occasional	Regular
	%	%	%	%
A	+15	+ 3	+ 7	−34
B	+19	+ 7	−14	−45
C1	+19	−2	−12	−47
C2	+29	−20	−33	−82
D	+23	+ 3	−47	−82
E	+ 3	+13	+ 6	−49

(Source: Institute of Practitioners in Advertising readership survey, 1977 to 1984)

The managerial and professional middle class increased its share of overall attendance from less than a fifth to around one-quarter (26.6%), and the lower white-collar workers increased from one-quarter to around one-third. White collar workers constituted around 60 per cent of the cinema audience, while the skilled and unskilled working class which had contributed over half of the audience in 1977 dropped to around one-third of the audience in 1983. Clearly a major force was at work. And before one jumps in to blame the video recorder, one should remember that ownership was relatively small among the working class during this period. Indeed, more white-collar workers had video recorders than did working-class householders.

As in the case of television, the myth of technological evolution which framed most people's initial thoughts about the relationship between film and video was misleading. As we show in detail in Chapter 3, video is closer to television, in terms of viewing habits and social experience, than it is to the cinema. To put it at its simplest we can state that cinema-goers are more likely to be video owners than non-cinema-goers. The reasons for owning a video do not preclude cinema attendance, and therefore again we have to look for social reasons to explain the decline rather than arguments about the quality of the films or the development of technology. The very success of a new technology is dependent on fertile conditions for its acceptance, and these fertile conditions may themselves spell death to another medium.

Conclusion

Cinema-attenders are people. Many commentators forget this simple fact. Going to the cinema is merely a small part of most people's lives. As a habit it is dependent on factors such as work, family, education, age and social class. As we have seen in this chapter, the decline of the cinema and the recent transformation in the class base of attendance are related to major social transformations in the ecology of cities, in levels and patterns of employment, changes in family patterns, changes in education, and the development of technologies for delivering moving images. Any real analysis of cinema attendance has to weave these strands together to prevent facile determinism or spurious hope. In the next chapter we show how the analysis of film viewing as a leisure activity greatly adds to our understanding of the role of film and cinema in people's lives.

CHAPTER 2

Leisure and the Cinema Audience

IN TOM STOPPARD's play, *Rosencrantz and Guildenstern
are Dead*, the characters, adrift in a boat, refuse to believe
in the existence of England, claiming that it is a 'conspiracy
of cartographers'. To refuse to believe in the reality of things
which might sink one's boat is understandable if the consequences of finding the place is one's death (as in the case of
Rosencrantz and Guildenstern), but the Humpty Dumpty-
like attempt to make the world conform to one's beliefs
(rather than the other way round) is dangerous for any
industry. Perhaps because films are powerful aesthetic experiences the film audience is often glamorised. Those who
subscribe to such an analysis probably believe that the social
analysis of the film audience is a conspiracy of demographers,
and yet, in one respect at least, going to the cinema is no
different from going to the zoo, the pub, a football match,
a concert, a dance or the final of an Elvis Presley look-
alike competition. It is a form of leisure and despite an
understandable desire to jump the gun and discuss aesthetic
preferences, visual pleasure or the one hundred and one other
things which make film audiences fascinating, the analysis of
cinema attendance must concentrate initially on cinema as a
leisure activity. After the audience is socially situated the
aesthetic dimension – the realm of pleasure – can be more
clearly understood. There might well be a mystical
communion between films and spectators, but, like the Virgin

Mary and the Poles, worship is more likely if social conditions are conducive.

What kind of leisure is cinema? Defining leisure causes all sorts of difficulties. Stanley Parker, the pioneer of leisure studies in Britain, points out that definitions tend to fall into three categories: residual, normative and mixed. Residual definitions divide the day up into various time/activity segments: sleeping, eating, working, etc. – the residue is leisure time. Normative definitions emphasise the quality of activities, which are not considered to be leisure activities unless they contribute to the well-being of the individual in some way. Mixed definitions accept the residual aspect of leisure, but they insist that certain normative assumptions about the quality of activities have to be included in order to round out the definition. (Parker 1986)

After World War II a consensus emerged around the idea that leisure was 'a good thing'. But in recent years the reappearance of mass unemployment, and the hitherto unknown experience of mass youth unemployment, has raised many questions about the role of leisure in late (or post-) industrial society. Some, like Glasser, regard leisure as an anaesthetic, a drug to fill the void left by the absence of clear goals and ambitions in the modern world. The mass society view of leisure is that the masses have abandoned themselves to television, jogging and Sony Walkmen. (Glasser 1970) Many Marxists would agree with Hargreaves that modern leisure is 'unique in its capacity to provide surrogate satisfaction for an alienated mass audience, while at the same time perpetuating its alienation and functioning as a means of political socialization into the hegemonic culture.' (1975: 60) In this view leisure is no different from work in the way that the working class relate to it. Leisure is the perpetuation of oppression by other means. It tantalizes the working class with a dream of freedom, but eventually they have to return to work (or the unemployment benefit office) on Monday morning. This reductionist view of leisure smacks of Brylcreem, Bovril, peaked caps and rickets; it is a sepia-coloured photograph, based in the past. Furthermore it is ultimately elitist; it treats the working class like automatons programmed by capitalism.

It would be unfair to say that every Marxist thinks this way. In the 1970s, under the impact of the Italian Communist Antonio Gramsci, British Marxists began to reformulate the idea of leisure. The Centre for Contemporary Cultural Studies in Birmingham emphasised the ways in which the working class resist the dominant culture. Working-class leisure was a way of negotiating the class struggle in the realm of culture. While the idea that the working class are consciously working away at the class struggle is a little optimistic, the Centre's approach is certainly an improvement on mass society theorists or old-fashioned Marxists. It is fundamental to our approach to leisure that people are regarded as active negotiators of leisure. Most people *are* perfectly aware of the ways that their background, education and employment structure their leisure and pleasure. The problem for most people is the cost of leisure, not its existence.

Although forced leisure seems a contradiction in terms, unemployment is challenging this view. Since the 1970s, millions of people in the industrialised world have been living with the consequences of a new industrial revolution which will possibly produce benefits such as shorter working hours, more holidays and better working conditions. But in the short-term many unemployed people – including around one million young people – have to fill in dog days. Commentators like Barry Sherman feel that we must have a leisure revolution to meet this challenge. (Sherman 1986) He argues that while we have to find ways to enlarge the work force, in the short-term we have to encourage those without conventional employment to escape the enervations of unemployment: we must ensure that leisure is qualitatively better. (Sherman 1986) Whatever the definitional problems, leisure is part of most people's lives, and as Sherman reminds us, it will become increasingly important as we move into the 21st century.

In order to understand film as leisure and to locate the future of film viewing we need a working definition. Fortunately, audiovisual entertainment leisure is not quite as difficult to define as the general concept. We take it to refer to non-work time in which people collectively or individually engage in audiovisual activities different from those which they are obliged to do, and from which they anticipate pleasure. With this working definition in mind we can outline four types of leisure: unconditional leisure, which is valued for its own sake; compensatory and recuperative leisure, which people do in order to rest and restore their energies; relational leisure, in which the social relationships are valued more than the pursuit itself (for example, a golf game with a client or going out with a boyfriend or girlfriend); finally, complementary leisure, which is a spillover from work (for example, English teachers reading novels, musicians going to a concert).

Cinema can fit into all of these frameworks. It is valued by a hard core of cinephiles as an end in itself, many people use it in order to relax and escape, most use it for relational purposes, and those involved in the industry use it for complementary or business reasons. We are not arguing that cinema is simply a way of killing time, but that most cinema attendances (as opposed to film-viewing) tell a story about social relationships rather than aesthetic choice. The relationship is the message. But, even though the relationship is the motivating factor, those who attend the cinema do so in preference to some other leisure activity. There is something in the audiovisual experience of the cinema which gives people pleasure, and if leisure is the skin of the cinema experience pleasure is its core. Therefore it is vital that we understand the importance of leisure in relation to the cinema, because without it we will have no understanding of the pleasures which films provide for their audiences.

We have argued that the decline in cinema attendance was a product of changes in the nature and extent of leisure, which, whilst they have not affected the popularity of film, have affected the forms of film-watching. When leisure time is scarce it is valued so highly that a premium is placed on doing something special with it, otherwise one has *wasted* the time. Work comes around again all too quickly. When leisure time is dramatically increased it becomes impossible to fill by distinct time-bounded activities and audiovisual entertainment is placed more firmly within everyday experience. Going out for such entertainment is a product of a special interest in, and need for, entertainment which is not based on the home.

In the rest of this chapter we demonstrate the intricate connections between people's everyday lives and their film viewing habits. The ideas for the chapter have emerged from our survey and should be interpreted as general statements and not universal truths. We do not want people to succumb to the false lure of statistics; for instance, when we say that cinema attendance declines with age, we mean that the majority of people over the age of 50 no longer go to the cinema: but, some still do. When we say that cinema-going is a young person's activity it is easy to believe that all young people go to the cinema whereas, in fact, around half of them do not. What we will try to do throughout this chapter is provide reasons for the majority tendency; for example, why slightly more than half of those between sixteen and twenty-nine attend the cinema. We hope that the reasons for the other half not going will become obvious in the analysis.

In 1986 there were around 1000 million viewings of films on video and hundreds of millions of viewings of films on television in the United Kingdom. Watching an entertainment film and gaining pleasure from it is primarily a home-based experience. Consider the cold fact that when people are asked where they *prefer* to watch films, the majority opt for seeing them as they appear on scheduled television, rather than watching tapes on a VCR or going to the cinema.

TABLE 11

Preferred medium for watching a feature film

N = 795

	Total	Age			Class			
		16–29	30–49	50+	AB	C1	C2	DE
	795	227	346	210	128	219	215	321
Cinema	31	39	31	21	43	38	27	20
VCR	22	31	26	6	14	20	27	24
Television	42	26	35	70	36	38	40	50
Don't know	6	4	9	2	7	4	7	6

Primarily, those who prefer to watch films on television and video do so for non-aesthetic reasons: freedom to choose when to watch; comfort; the chance to re-wind (see Chapter 3 for a more detailed analysis) and, further down the line, cost. For the cinema-goer the main benefits are aesthetic and social: the quality of sound and image, the large screen and the indefinable quality of 'atmosphere'.

Social forces structure the preference for one medium over another. For instance, only one in six of the upper middle class prefer watching films on a VCR compared to one-quarter of the semi-skilled working class. Furthermore, fully 70 per cent of those over the age of 50 prefer to watch films on television compared to one-quarter of those between 16 and 29.

Leisure behaviour is not necessarily based on these preferences: nearly half of those attending the cinema last year preferred to watch films on television and video. Furthermore

TABLE 12

Reasons for preference

Cinema N = 243

	%
Atmosphere	56
Large screen	45
Better sound	24
Better picture	19
Like to go out	15
Darkness	3
Crowd	3
More comfort	1

VCR N = 176

	%
Watch when want	63
Chance to rewind	37
No need to go out	17
Choice of films	7
Cheaper	7

Television N = 33

	%
Convenient	48
No need to go out	42
Cheaper	22
Better quality	4

(These were multiple choice questions, thus adding up to more than 100%)

the mere possession of a VCR does not automatically result in a preference for that medium; only 40 per cent of video-owners prefer the VCR, with one-third opting for cinema and around one-quarter preferring television. In order to understand how preferences lead to behaviour (or vice versa) we have to look at the ways in which films fit into the structure of peoples lives, and in particular how people's relationship with the different audiovisual media change as they grow older and/or acquire family responsibilities.

1   Cinema and the Life-Cycle

Insight into the relationship between life-cycle and leisure can be gained by isolating aspects of people's lives which push them toward leisure activities outside of the home, and the types of pull which leisure activities can exert to channel the desire for activity. An example of a push factor would be the presence of children during the school holidays or at weekends. The demand for leisure to be taken outside of the home grows during these periods, but it might not be fulfilled in a structured sense unless leisure possibilities are clearly established. Examples of the latter are a blockbuster film, a favourite soccer team having a run in the cup, or a pregnant giant panda at London Zoo. These shape, but in general do not cause, the demand for leisure.

This push-pull relationship illuminates the differences between those who *sometimes* attend the cinema, the pool of attenders, and those who *regularly* attend. The former consists of those who attended the cinema at least once a year, which according to our figures was one in four of the adult population in 1984 – around ten million people. The bulk of those in the pool went only a couple of times during 1984, but there was a small but significant group of regular attenders who went once a month or more, and who provided around two-thirds of all attendances at the cinema.

As can be seen from the following tables there are some key differences between the cinema audience and the national population. For instance single people double their representation in the pool of attenders, and increase by a multiplier of four among regular attenders; the proportion of married couples drops by over one-fifth in the pool and by around two-thirds among the regular attenders. It is interesting to note in passing that the proportion of those who are widowed drops from 6 per cent of the population as a whole to 1 per cent of the pool; this has serious implications for the cinema among an ageing population.

TABLE 13(A)

Cinema attendance in Great Britain: 1984

N = 795

a) By marital status

	Adult Population	Pool*	Regular**
Weighted Base	795	207	54
	%	%	%
Single	18	36	74
Married	70	56	26
Separated/Divorced	4	4	
Widowed	6	1	

b) By age

	Adult Population	Pool*	Regular**
16–20	9	24	
21–24	7	10	
25–34	26	30	
35–44	23	23	
45–54	11	8	
55–64	11	3	
65+	11	2	
16–29	29	48	80
30–49	26	30	13
40+	44	21	6

* Pool = Those who attended at least once in 1984
** Regular = Those who attended once a month or more

Although these figures relate to 1984, the update of our survey in Spring 1986 (see Table 13b) and subsequent market research on the behaviour of the adult audience confirm that the structure of the pool and the regular audience is markedly different. Those who go once a month are overwhelmingly single and between the ages of 16 and 24, whereas the pool has a more even distribution. Even so, the pool shows that the one-fifth of the population over the age of 55 make up a mere 5 per cent of the pool, and that the over 55s are virtually non-existent among the regular audience. On the other hand teenagers represent one in ten of the adult population but make up one-quarter of the pool and around four-fifths of the regular audience. Social class is evenly distributed in the pool whereas the semi-skilled working class are under-represented and lower white-collar workers over-represented in the regular audience.

Clearly there are forces at work on cinema attendance beyond the quality of films and cinemas. Our central point

TABLE 13(B)

Cinema attendance 1986

		Age					Class			
	Total	15–24	25–34	35–44	45–64	55+	AB	C1	C2	DE
	1016	201	178	148	133	356	168	225	308	316
	%	%	%	%	%	%	%	%	%	%
Never	68	30	64	60	82	90	62	64	63	80
Once	10	12	15	17	6	5	15	9	14	6
2–3 times	12	27	13	16	8	3	13	14	13	8
4–5 times	3	9	3	4	3	1	3	5	3	2
6–10 times	3	11	2	2	–	–	5	2	4	2
11–20 times	2	7	2	1	–	–	1	3	2	1
Over 20	1	4	1	1	1	–	1	3	–	–
Don't know	–	–	–	–	–	–	–	–	–	–

is that the needs and interests which create leisure behaviour in general also lead to a particular type of consumption of cinema. There are three different types of cinema attenders: married couples with children, the courting couple and the unattached. These different groups are by and large not affected in their cinema-going habits by films in the cinemas in and of themselves. Nothing short of a miracle will turn a working-class father of two children of pre-school age into someone who attends the cinema on a regular basis. An examination of the consumption of visual entertainment must be approached through the analysis of work, the home, and family types.

There is, for example, a strong seasonal bias in cinema attendance, with peak periods during the school holidays at Christmas and the summer. It is during these two periods that the push factors which create the conditions for leisure demand are at their height. People have holidays, and if they are parents they have children who want to do things. In these circumstances cinema is more likely to be seen as an attractive option. The effect of children is such that those with older children between the ages of 5 and 14 are proportionally over-represented in the pool. Parents maintain their connection to the cinema into their thirties because of, rather than *in spite of*, their children. This can be seen in Table 14, where it is obvious that children are the catalyst for the cinema visits of a large proportion of adults.

Relationships within households are dynamic. As children grow older they acquire and demand more independence. This affects the structure of family relationships and has deep implications for leisure patterns. Some households are characterised by *open* leisure relationships; they have centrifugal leisure patterns, each member of the household pursuing leisure independently from each other outside the home. *Closed* households are marked by centripetal leisure patterns where most leisure is shared and centred on the home.

TABLE 14

Who chooses the film

N = 235

	Total	Have children	Unmarried
Weighted Base	235	98	27
	%	%	%
Respondent	32	23	49
Children	28	41	2
Husband/wife	20	36	–
Boy/girlfriend	12	1	40
Friends (same sex)	11	2	12
Friends (opposite sex)	6	3	8

(This was a multiple choice question and therefore the columns adds up to more than 100%.)

Think yourself into a family: husband 25, wife 22, joint income of £10,000. Before marriage both regularly went out to the pub with friends, to discos, parties and, once a month, the cinema. During engagement the amount of time spent with friends declined as they began saving for the wedding and the house. They continued to attend the cinema because it was a relatively cheap form of entertainment and they could escape the pressures of being in the home with parents and young children. When they married their leisure surplus was squeezed still further and they began to spend most of their time at home, both for financial reasons and because they were committed to the idea and the experience of the home. Cinema attendance declined to once or twice a year.

Eight years later they have two children, aged 5 and 7. Both are on holiday from school. The eldest has an ET doll, a poster of Han Solo on the wall, and a Superman costume. The youngest has Care Bears and a Wooky poster. The parents have to find something that they can do as a family in order to keep the children occupied, but also because they enjoy the feeling of being together as a family and the pleasure of their children is extremely important. They ask the children what they want to do; both cry: 'Son of ET, please!'

Ten years on, the oldest son is 17, the younger 15. Neither of them can stand the sight of the other, and they are constantly at odds with their parents. The 17-year-old has a girlfriend and spends a great deal of time out of the house with her and his friends. He goes to the cinema once a month. The younger son has friends around to watch films on the video-recorder (VCR). The parents have stopped going to the cinema since the children no longer want them to go with them. They rent a feature film once a week.

Think yourself into other families which do not conform to this pattern; say, a family where the father is unemployed, or a single-parent family, an extended family, or an Asian family. The rhythms of their lives and the changing patterns affect their leisure. And when leisure is affected then the relationship to the cinema and to film is affected.

Certain members of the family are more likely to interact than others. A husband and wife will spend more time together than a young teenage brother and sister; two brothers of roughly the same age will interact more regularly than brothers with a large age difference, but these patterns will change during the life-cycle.

The family cycle provides for different types of leisure but the meaning the family has for its individual members also affects the ways in which leisure is channelled. The family is more important for a 5-year-old than for a 15-year-old; it expects more integration from a 10-year-old than a 20-year-old; and, in certain traditional regions of the country, it is still expected that the daughters spend more time with the family than the sons. A family in which most household tasks are shared between both sexes will be more leisure-integrated than a traditional family with strict divisions of household labour.

We have to look at the structural pressures which produce the open and closed patterns of household leisure: age of adults, number and age of children, availability and cost of leisure facilities and income play their part. For instance, the development of VCRs has facilitated the extensive use of film as collective entertainment in closed households. As a result of this, film has become re-appropriated as everyday, habitual leisure for these families. Therefore when they are pushed out of the home the cinema will have a hard time in attracting them. Films are not special enough to mark the occasion which generated the out-of-home activity.

It is apparent from our evidence that the act of choosing which film to see is itself structured by the reasons for going to see it. If one is only going in order to satisfy the children then the children are the most important determinant in choosing. Something of the importance of children can be seen in the fact that only 28 per cent of married people say that they actually prefer to watch films in the cinema. We are therefore left with the strong impression that marriage does not coincide with regular cinema-going. Even when the push and pull factors combine to get married people into the cinema, in the majority of cases they themselves have not chosen the films that they have come to see.

This is not the case with the most important group amongst the regular attenders, which comprises those unmarried people between the ages of 18 and 24 who have a steady relationship. Just over half of this group attended the cinema in 1984, and it is the only group in which the majority claimed to go to the cinema. As we can see from Table 13 they are also the most regular cinema attenders. It should be remembered of course that almost half of this group did not attend the cinema even once during 1984. There is no simple causal relationship between being young and attached, and attending the cinema. Other factors come into play: physical distance from a cinema, range of other interests, level of education, unemployment and family responsibilities, to name a few.

The basic reason for the level of attendance among this group is the push factor of having to get out of the house, or having to find a leisure pursuit which fits in with the demand to see one another regularly. This is reflected in the fact that 63 per cent of young couples went to the cinema only with their boy/girlfriend. An interesting aspect of their attendance is its ritualistic character; half of them claim they prefer to attend the cinema at the weekend, which would seem to indicate that cinema-going is still part of the ritual of courting and remains a safe bet for a night out. Furthermore, these young couples tend to integrate cinema into a general night out: two-thirds went to the pub before or after the cinema, one-fifth for a meal, and one-third had some kind of take-away meal.

One should not imagine, however, that our courting couples are especially enamoured of the cinema. They want regular, cheap entertainment and therefore attend the cinema regularly, but they still feel that cinema is too expensive for what it offers them. Even for this captive audience, where the pull and push factors are operating at their most powerful to attract people to the cinema, they are neither satisfied with what they receive, nor are they committed to the cinema as an activity or experience. This partly explains the marked decline in attendance when couples marry or live together and no longer need regular nights out away from the parental home.

The third group, after young marrieds and courting couples, are those between the ages of 16 and 29 who are unattached. Although they are roughly the same age as those with a regular relationship they have different motivations for attending the cinema. Around two-fifths attend the cinema in a year. They do not attend as regularly as those with a steady partner – 15 per cent attended at least once a month in 1984; double the figure for married people and around half of that for unmarried couples.

Age is by far the most important factor influencing regular cinema attendance. The stark reality of cinema attendence is that 22 per cent of those aged between 16 and 29 who are part of the pool of cinema attenders attended once a month or more, compared to a mere 5 per cent of those over 30. Although the latter are an important part of the cinema audience they simply do not go regularly enough to provide a stable basis for a successful industry. This can be further established from the fact that whilst only one-third of those under 30 who are part of the pool of attenders visit the cinema less than four times a year, seven out of ten of those over 30 go one to three times a year. These figures are further confirmed by the number of times that people attended over the four-month period prior to the survey: 15 per cent of the 16–29 age group had been one or more times, compared to 6 per cent of those between 30 and 39, and only 3 per cent of those over 40.

Age also makes a difference to the level of commitment to the cinema. Young people are much more assertive when choosing which film to see; around half claimed to have chosen the film themselves, whereas less than one-third of 30–49-year-olds claimed to have done so. The children and spouses of married people are more likely to choose which film to attend. Life-cycle dictates both levels of attendance and the commitment to the very act of choosing the film.

When adolescence opens up the household it also affects the ritual of cinema attendance. Young people are strong weekend attenders; around half claim that they prefer to go at the weekend, compared to only one-quarter of the 29–39 age group and one-fifth of the over-40s. Most of the reasons given by the 16–29 group centre around the symbolic and physical importance of the weekend. Around one-third agree that 'freedom to do what one wants' is their reason for preferring the weekend to attend. The over-30s are more concerned with boredom than freedom: one quarter said that they attended during the week because they had 'nothing else to do'. Cinema is not an *event* for this group in the same way that it is for those who prefer going at the weekend.

The creation of the event is obviously of central importance to most young people. Attending the cinema is contained within the overall event of 'going out'. Only one-fifth of them did not go either to the pub or to have a meal; in contrast the vast majority of the 30–39-year-old group simply went to the cinema and did nothing else during that evening.

It is interesting, considering that young people are more inclined to treat the cinemas as an event (although the event is probably the evening out and not the cinema itself), that they are not convinced that the cinema is good value for money: six out of ten do not consider the cinema good value, compared to four out of ten 30–49-year-olds. Furthermore, when asked which types of leisure facility were most important for local communities, a cinema came well down the list, with only 10-per cent nominating it as important, compared to 43 per cent who opted for a pub, 45 per cent

TABLE 15

Cinema good value for money compared to other entertainments

N = 386

	16–29	30–39	40+
Weighted Base	186	118	82
	%	%	%
Good value	47	56	51
Bad value	31	26	28
About the same	20	15	15
Don't know	2	3	5

for a sports centre, 13 per cent for a disco, 12 per cent for a swimming pool, and 12 per cent for a chippie. The need for a cinema is not branded on the hearts of the nation's youth, despite the assumptions of the film industry.

The notion of what is good value for money is related to reasons why people are prepared to spend money on a cinema ticket. If they buy the ticket to be with their boyfriend or girlfriend, and they have already seen two of the three films at the local triplex, which means that they are forced to watch a film in the smallest and dingiest of the three theatres, then the experience will not seem to be good value. If on the other hand, someone only attends once or twice a year, and they go to a well-publicised film, shown in the best local cinema, then that person is more inclined to view the cinema as good value.

2   Social Class and the Cinema

Although both academics and laymen presume a relationship between taste and class, one must beware lest class analysis blind us to the complexities of occupational experience. A shop-floor worker in a large factory will share a similar routine to that of middle management in the factory, while a forestry worker, a craftsman, or a farm worker in the same income bracket as the shop-floor worker will have very different attitudes to routine and bureaucracy.

Some films are clearly divided in terms of their audience; for example, *Superman III* was split 66 per cent to 31 per cent in favour of the manual working class, while *Gandhi* was split 67 per cent to 33 per cent in favour of white-collar workers and the middle class. No great surprise here, one would think. But the Cinema and Video Industry Audience Research report from which the above example was taken shows that around half of those in middle-class occupations attended 'mass' entertainment films, rather than 'art' films.

Within the middle class it seems that teachers, lecturers, social workers and others in the 'caring' professions prefer art house films, whereas middle management in commercial companies prefer straightforward commercial films.

TABLE 16

Cinema attendance by class

	Adult Population	Pool	Regular
Weighted Base	795	207	54
	%	%	%
AB	16	22	17
CI	28	30	37
C2	27	26	19
DE	29	22	26

(A: Upper-middle class (mostly old professions); B: middle class (lower or new professions, e.g. teachers, social workers, middle management); CI: White-collar workers; C2: Skilled working class; DE: Unskilled working class and those at lower levels of subsistence.)

Class also affects the ritual of cinema-going. The working class still prefers to go at the weekend: the idea of a 'night out' will take a long time to die. Less than one in ten of those in professions or white-collar occupations prefer the weekend, or go to the cinema because it is a 'night out'. Their lives are not circumscribed by drudgery in the same way, and therefore their leisure time is more flexible. The lower working class also relates cinema to relieving boredom: around one-quarter of them attending the cinema claimed that they attended at the weekend because they had 'nothing else to do'.

As well as this somewhat traditional idea of the weekend, the working class cling also to the idea of the local cinema: nine out of ten prefer to watch films in a local cinema compared to only six out of ten professionals. Because most young professionals spend their working lives outside of their local area they probably less committed to the neighbourhood as a location for leisure activities. The working class in fact claim that they would attend more if the cinema were closer to them whereas the majority of middle-class respondents claim that the location of the cinema would make little difference. These echoes of cinema's past are fascinating. They demonstrate that there is a deep but buried feeling for the idea of the well-established local cinema, where one could have a good time surrounded by people one knows. Unfortunately people are also nostalgic for the tenement slums of Glasgow, but no one in their right mind would go back there. Nostalgia will not bring the cinema back to life.

Thus far we have shown how cinema attendance emerges out of people's everyday lives. We have demonstrated that the home provides the initial framework for the development of leisure patterns. These patterns, however, are altered by income (those on subsistence incomes seldom attend the cinema); education (further education leads to an increase in cinema-attendance); employment (white-collar workers are more regular attenders) and geography (many people simply have no access to a cinema). Moving from the general audience for commercial cinema to the audience for specialist films throws this complex interaction into sharper focus.

3   A Touch of Class: the Audience for Specialist Films

There is always an element of spelling out the obvious in survey analysis. Thus telling the managers of specialist cinemas that they have a predominantly middle-class cinephile audience is like informing the manager of Glasgow Rangers that his supporters are Protestants – it is one of the self-evident facts of cultural life. There are around 60 cinemas in the UK which show specialist films, generally foreign-language and independent British and US productions (see the box office list below). Around 37 of these cinemas are supported by the British Film Institute and form the Regional Film Theatre Consortium. These are, by and large, the main source of non-mainstream films outside London. Unsurprisingly the audience for the RFTs is different from the average audience for commercial cinema. Most

CHART 1

The RFT box-office top ten 1986

Film Title	Net box office £	Admissions	Renter	Country of Origin
Room With a View	1,00,647	64056	Enterprise	UK
Kiss of the Spider Woman	91,547	58,558	Palace	USA/ Brazil
No Surrender	54,064	33,237	Palace	UK
After Hours	44,674	28,209	Col-Cannon -Warner	US
Ran	39,432	25,132	Premier	Japan/ France
Death in a French Garden	36,161	22,703	Artificial Eye	France
Sid and Nancy	35,927	23,127	Palace	UK
Desert Hearts	29,803	19,148	Mainline	US
Caravaggio	26,841	17,356	BFI	UK
Vagabonde	16,321	10,865	BFI/ Electric	France
Love Letters	13,310	8,551	ICA/Blue Dolphin	US
Police	9,386	5,953	Artificial Eye	France
Revolution	7,437	4,951	Col-Cannon -Warner	UK/ Norway

CHART 2

London specialist box-office 1986

	£
Room With a View	1,238,291
Kiss of the Spider Woman	348,183
After Hours	320,815
Ran	279,549
Desert Hearts	165,578
Caravaggio	147,781
Sid and Nancy	138,062
Death in a French Garden	129,617
Revolution	87,369
No Surrender	65,652
Vagabonde	39,458
Love Letters	36,674
Police	37,454

(Source: J. Gerson and S. Boxall, 'Opening the Box Office' (BFI internal document, February 1987))

importantly, the RFT audience attends the cinema more regularly; furthermore, they are deeply committed to the cinema as an art form.

It is quite remarkable to discover a group of people who remain committed to the cinema to the extent of attending once a week or more. If the social analysis outlined in this chapter is correct we should be able to discover some common denominator which will enable us to identify the reason why this audience is committed to the cinema.

One way to make judgements about this is to look at the social and demographic profile of the audience. This is different from the general audience in several important respects, most importantly class and education. Over one-third of the RFT audience is in full-time education, and if we add in the number of lecturers and teachers then over half of the audience are connected to full-time education. There is clearly something about an arts- or social science-based education which leads to the perception of cinema as an art form. The concern with a 'humanist' cinema (in the broadest sense) seems to pervade the concerns of students and lecturers.

TABLE 17

The best way to watch a feature film

	General Population	Age 18–29	RFT
Base	795	227	2187
	%	%	%
Cinema	31	39	89
VCR	22	31	3
Television	42	26	3
Don't know	6	4	5
	100	100	100

TABLE 18 A

Regularity of attendance of RFT audience in 3-month period

N = 2187

	At RFT	At Commercial Cinema
	%	%
1–3 visits	39	50
4–5 visits	24	18
7 or more	22	12
Not at all	16	20

TABLE 18 B

Regularity of attendance of general audience in 4-month period

N = 388

	%
1–3 visits	49
4 or more visits	10
Did not attend	43

The cultural leanings of the RFT audience can be seen in their newspaper readership. One need say no more than that 57 per cent of the RFT audience read *The Guardian*. A further 19 per cent read *The Times* and the *Daily Telegraph*, whereas the tabloids can muster only 21 per cent between them. This bias is repeated in radio listening: one-third of the RFT audience listen to Radio 4 (double the figure for the

TABLE 19

Class

RFT		Commercial Audience	
	%		%
AB Education	17	AB	22 (17)
AB Professional	17	CI	30 (37)
AB Commercial	9	C2	26 (19)
CI	17	DE	22 (26)
C2	5		
Students	36		

(The figures in brackets refer to the regular, as opposed to the total, audience.)

population as a whole), whereas only 4 per cent listen to Radio 2, which is normally listened to by one quarter of the population.

The other major point of difference between the average commercial audience and the specialist one is the latter's commitment to entertainment activities. The specialist film

TABLE 20

RFT audience's attendance at other entertainments

	Classical Concert	Theatre	Pop/Art Concert	Art Galleries	Night Clubs/ Discos
N =	2223	2283	2215	2266	2230
	%	%	%	%	%
1–3 times	28	43	35	41	26
4–6 times	8	20	12	20	12
7 or more	7	21	11	20	30
Not at all	57	16	41	18	32

audience is media-rich: they are theatre-goers, art gallery habitués, disco maniacs and clubbers. The commercial audience seems less concerned with such frenetic activity.

Attendance at specialist cinemas is clearly connected to class and to type of education. And yet, despite this connection, and regardless of the commitment of RFT audiences to the cinema, they stop attending the cinema at precisely the same age as young people attending the commercial cinema. In other words, the social forces which bring about the decline in cinema attendance are as powerful among those who believe in the cinema as they are among those who use it as just another leisure facility.

There is a considerable drop-off in attendances among the RFT audience after 35, and, like the general cinema audience,

TABLE 21

Age

RFT Audience		Commercial Cinema Audience	
N = 2140		N = 795	
	%		%
Under 15	1		
16–25	47	16–29	48 (80)
26–35	29	30–39	30 (13)
36–45	12	40+	21 (6)
46–60	7		
Over 60	3		

(The figures in brackets are for those among the general audience who go 4 or more times a year.)

TABLE 22

Who respondent attended the cinema with

	General	Age 18–29	RFT
Base	795	100	2119
	%	%	%
Husband/wife	40	26	20
Other member of family (including children)	61	24	3
Boyfriend/girlfriend	14	30	25
Friends same sex	13	18	28
Friends opposite sex	7	11	9
No one	4	7	16

(This was multiple choice and therefore adds up to more than 100% in some cases.)

the bulk of attendances are by the 16–29 age group. Clearly the factors which push people out of the house at this age are as important to the RFT audience as they are to the general audience. The desire for cinema does not seem to survive the ageing process even among those most committed to the experience of the big screen.

Finally, the specialist cinema audience replicates the commercial audience insofar as cinema attendance is primarily a social activity. Those who attend tend to do so with their boyfriend or girlfriend. It remains an activity intimately related to the rituals of courtship, regardless of the interest the couples have in the films which they go to see.

This part of the research has demonstrated that even in the heartland of film audiences – the specialist cinema – social forces clearly operate to structure and then undermine cinema attendance. If this is so, then even this most special of cases confirms our thesis that cinema must be treated first and foremost as a leisure pursuit.

Conclusion

Surveys are 'snapshots' of history, particularly during periods of rapid social change. The cinema audience was at the end of a long period of decline when our survey took place; but, as we have shown, the processes which underly audience levels have been the same since the war. Primarily cinema-attendance is shaped by people's life cycles, but despite this type of social analysis certain films will come along to challenge even non-cinema attenders. *ET*, for example, brought people to the cinema who had not been in years. Unfortunately for the industry a cinema-event like *ET* or *Gone With the Wind* happens once in a blue moon, and seldom leads to major behavioural changes in cinema attendance. It is important to understand the nature of taste, and why films are such a popular form of entertainment. In Chapter 4 we will deal with this in great detail, but first of all we will turn to the phenomenon of video, which turned the experience of film on its head in the space of two years.

CHAPTER 3

Welcome to the Videodrome

VIDEO EXPLODED on to the British media scene. In the space of a few years in the early 1980s it advanced from a suspect youth – when it was the preserve of porn merchants, shady corner dealers and shift workers – into a rather stodgy middle-age: one moment a luxury, the next commonplace.

The second great haemorrhage in the cinema audience happened at the same time as VCR sales exploded. Once again this led to darkly pessimistic thoughts about the inevitable decline in the cinema and its replacement by a more modern technology which could deliver a greater choice of films more cheaply. The prophets of doom were shown to be wrong when cinema attendances picked up in 1985 and 1986 despite continued growth in VCR sales and videogram rentals. Furthermore, market research exposed the simple fact that those with VCRs were more likely to be cinema attenders than those without. Once again, facile technological determinism failed to explain the facts.

The pundits were wrong because they did not grasp the essential point about video: *a night in watching a video is not a night out spent at home.* The structural and personal reasons for out-of-home leisure remain in existence, and they protect the cinema despite the possibility of watching relatively new feature films on video. Although feature films are the main product for cinema and video, this disguises the profound differences between the two media: video is closer to television than it is to the cinema.

In this chapter we examine the reasons why video-watching and levels of cinema attendance are virtually unconnected. In particular we demonstrate that the reasons people give for pursuing these activities are entirely different, and that video (or for that matter, a subscription film channel) has to be treated as a very different film experience from that of the cinema. As we shall see, watching a video does not recreate the cinema in the home.

1 The Growth of Video

Video slipped into the lives of around one-third of the British population between 1982 and 1984, bringing with it predictions of doom and gloom for the television and cinema industries. Initially these predictions looked as if they were

TABLE 23

Hardware figures

Year	Volume (000s)(a)	Proportion of adults with VCR in household (b)
		%
1978	65	
1979	115	
1980	350	
1981	970	7
1982	2030	16
1983	2180	26
1984	1505	33
1985	1620	40
1986	1950	51

(Sources: (a) Consumer uptake: British Radio and Electrical Manufacturers Association (b) British Videogramme Association.)

coming true. The growth in television advertising revenue slowed down in 1984 as, apparently, audiences declined; furthermore, cinema audiences dropped to less than one visit per head of the population. If video was not God it was certainly on the way to being king.

As it grew the ownership profile changed. In the early 1980s the Economist Intelligence Unit suggested that around one-third of VCR owners were middle and upper middle-class (AB), who make up around one-sixth of the population. Similarly our own research found higher penetration in middle-class and skilled working-class homes than in other socio-economic groups.

TABLE 24

UK video market profile 1981

Age	%
18–24	19
25–34	37
35–44	31
45–54	9
55–65	3
65+	1
Household	**%**
Adults only	44
Adults/children (2–14)	43
Adults/infants (under 2)	5
Adult/children/infants	8
Socio-economic Group	**%**
AB	35
C1	29
C2	27
DE	9

(Source: EIU 1982)

TABLE 25

UK video profile 1984/5

N = 795

Age	%
16–29	33
30–49	56
50+	10

Household penetration	%
Adults only	24
Children (under 5)	42
Children (5–14)	43

Class penetration	%
AB	41
C1	31
C2	43
DE	24

(Source: BRU)

Although these two surveys are not strictly comparable one important development should be noted, namely the rapid growth of the VCR in skilled working-class and lower middle-class homes. Another important development was the rapid penetration of the VCR into households with children. Far from being an individualistic medium, with one viewer watching a film, video was a family medium first and foremost. It fitted into the collective and individual life of family members.

With cinema attendances hovering around 70 million in 1986, it comes as something of a shock to realise that there were around 350 million rentals of feature films in 1986; furthermore, on average three people watch each rented film, which gives a total of 1,050 million viewings. The great days of film watching have returned; but why is the film industry reluctant to hang out the flags?

TABLE 26

Official sales and rentals

	Value (£)
1983	283,000,000
1985	306,000,000
1986	435,000,000

(Source: British Videogramme Association)

The film industry's reluctance to accept video is partly financial – the pirate market drained off much of the potential profit in the early years (around 30% in 1983) – but, the real issue is that at heart, deep down, most film-makers want to see their product on big screens with Dolby sound. Furthermore, most film-makers understandably want a large and appreciative audience enraptured by the occasion. The problem is that this desire for the cinema obscures the pleasures which people receive from films. Quite simply, films are so popular as a form of mass entertainment that the setting or presentation does not unduly affect the pleasure gained: 80 per cent of our respondents claimed: 'If a film is good I don't mind where I watch it.'

This sentiment is central to the future of the film industry. It shows that the cinema has to be demystified, and cultural snobbery put to flight, if the industry is to address cultural and technical developments in the 1990s. It is understandable that the exhibition chains are concerned by the decline in attendance, but the emotional intensity of those advocating the protection of cinema is unparalleled in modern business. The promotional effort of British Film Year, for example, was entirely understandable as a marketing campaign, but it seemed like a moral crusade: a cry to the masses to renew their faith in film by returning to the place of true worship – the cinema.

At an aesthetic level the 'true believers' are probably correct. A 70 mm print in a large comfortable cinema creates the best conditions for the projection and reception of images and sounds, just as seeing El Greco's 'Purification of the Temple' at the National Gallery is infinitely superior to a blurry 3″ × 2″ reproduction. On the other hand, seeing a 35 mm print three months into its run in a city centre triplex is an awful experience by any standards. It is a bit like seeing an El Greco after someone had spent three months putting varnish on it. The defenders of the faith would have difficulty in judging this an experience superior to a reasonable quality video.

Many elements go into the statement 'the best way to see a film is at the cinema'. Crucially, as we have consistently pointed out, film is judged by its relation to the structure of people's lives and the meaning of their leisure time. When they say that they prefer to watch a film in the home they are asserting the primacy of the home in their evaluation of the pleasure of the film.

Advocates for cinema claim that despite the problems of dwindling audiences the cinema remains 'the best place to watch a film'. This view takes a personal preference and translates it into a general theory of pleasure. Furthermore, it mystifies the relationship between films and audiences. Although on the basis of perceptual psychology it is possible to make a case that the 70 mm print shown in a darkened room is objectively a better experience, social psychology would point to other conditions which create pleasure: whom you are with is as important as what you are seeing. Therefore, although 31 per cent of the population believe that cinema is the best way to watch a feature film, two-thirds opt for video and television. Having a video does not of itself lead to the rejection of the cinema; indeed only 40 per cent of video-owners prefered watching feature films on a VCR. Furthermore those with a video were *more* likely to nominate the cinema as their favourite medium.

TABLE 27

The best way to watch a feature film

N = 795

| | | Video Ownership | |
	Total	Yes	No
Weighted Base	795	270	525
	%	%	%
In the cinema	31	33	29
On a VCR at home	22	40	13
On TV at home	42	22	52
Don't know/no answer	6	6	6

The effect of video on the UK media scene is a little like the emergence of the Liberal-SDP Alliance in British politics. Just as the three-party political system has added new complications to the previously simple antagonism between Labour and Conservative voters, so video has confused the choice between home-based audiovisual entertainment (television) and out-of-home audiovisual entertainment (cinema). Video has to compete with the home-based nature of television viewing and the social aspects of going to the cinema, and this leads to a confusion as to whether people really prefer the VCR over the other two. For instance, only 28 per cent of married people prefer watching films on video compared to over half of single people with a steady relationship. On the surface this looks as if single people prefer the VCR more than married couples. But if one builds into the equation the fact that nearly half of married couples prefer watching films on television, compared to only one-fifth of unmarried couples, we can see that married people are in fact nominating the home as their favoured place for watching films, while single people are saying that they want choice in what they watch.

The length and strength of relationships is at the heart of preferring one medium over another. This is reflected in the reasons people give for preferring the VCR.

TABLE 28

Reasons for preferring video

N = 176

	Total
	%
Freedom to watch when you want	63
Chance to stop/rewind	37
Don't need to go out	17
Choice of films	7
Cheaper	7
Other	6
Don't know	2

(Multiple choice adds up to more than 100%.)

Contrary to popular myth, cost and choice are not the primary reasons for preferring video. People like the freedom to choose when and how they watch films. Stopping the film because the phone rings or friends come around is a simple practical bonus which the VCR adds to film viewing, but the rewind and stop facilities are more important than this. For example, when people do not understand a section of a film they go back and watch it again, and if they have a favourite clip they replay it. This is a different way to watch a film.

Stopping the film and breaking the narrative, or rewinding and repeating the narrative, break all the rules of watching a film in the cinema, but the experience should not be devalued for that reason. These 'rules' are the product of a particular period when films had to fit the strictures of a public culture. The cinema was the only place to see a film and the rules of public culture dictated that no one person had the right to influence how several hundred others should view a film. Consequently, films had to flow in a continous narrative. But how many people read books in this way? Books are put down at bedtime or read over lunch; the boring bits in the middle are sometimes skipped; the end is read first; favourite passages are pored over. The rules of reading are entirely different from hearing a written text read in public, but they can lead to a richer understanding of the work.

One final consideration should put the nail in the coffin of the argument that cinema is the best place to watch a film. By the year 2000 it is highly likely that people will be watching films which will be technically equivalent to 35 mm prints, on 3 ft wide flat screens *in their homes*. Will the cinema still be the best place to see a film in the age of high-definition television?

Just because cinema was the original home of film does not make it the best place to see film anymore than going to a football ground is the best place to watch soccer. You might 'feel' the game better if you go to the ground, indeed you will see more off-the-ball action, and perhaps understand the context of certain crucial moves, but you will see the crucial moves more clearly if you watch them on television. Furthermore, by watching slow motion replays you will better appreciate the technical aspects of the move. All this without racist chants, someone standing on your toes or having to eat disgusting pies at half-time. Just as we can no longer argue that the national sports are better if watched at the sports stadium so an analysis of video must steer clear of elitist assumptions about the quality of certain aesthetic experiences. Equally it must avoid simplistic populist arguments that video is the people's art simply because there are rewind and freeze-frame buttons on a video recorder. Cinema and video are different experiences, equally valid and equally cherished by the majority of the population.

We are not claiming that cinema should be abandoned in favour of video and television. At present the cinema still affords certain film-makers with a talent for the large canvas the best possible location to display their product. But historically artists have never controlled the conditions of reception for their work and these confines have resulted in a creative dynamic between the outlet for display and the type of work in which artists engage.

The sheer size of Renaissance churches and palaces allowed the artist scope for glorious expositions of mythological and religious themes, and the disappearance of grand houses has cut artists off from a class of private patrons who demanded size as a function of space (although corporate patrons occasionally demand something monstrous for the foyer of their latest office block). Few would say that art itself has suffered as a result of the demise of the aristocratic patron. Techniques have continued to develop, major artists still emerge, the exploration of major themes remains the driving force behind the work of many: size alone is not the issue. The pleasure and/or enlightenment which people gain from the small canvas is as important as the grandiloquence of a canvas made to fit a wall. Similarly the large frame may be disappearing for the film-maker, but the small screen remains a challenge which film-makers have to face. Cinema may be technically the best place to see *Lawrence of Arabia*, but the majority of films pumped out by Hollywood's fiction factories are not quite so demanding. The public understands the difference between cinematic films like *Star Wars*, and run-of-the-mill films which they can watch on video without the feeling of having missed something.

The popularity of television and video is related to the meaning people give to their lives and those meanings now tend to exclude the cinema as a regular activity. The changed social circumstances of individuals and families (particularly among the urban working class) has been responsible for poor cinema attendance. Quite simply, television, and now video, have fitted in with the broad structural changes that have altered the individual's relationship to leisure. In this respect video is closer to television than it is to the cinema.

2 Video: a Different Type of Television?

We have shown that the relationship between the cinema and video is by no means simple. In this section we examine the relationship between video and television, showing that the experience of video is closer to, though distinct from, television, and that people watch video films for the same reasons as they watch television.

The rapid increase in the purchase and rental of VCRS

TABLE 29

Reasons for acquiring a video

N = 391

	Total	AB	C1	C2	DE
Weighted Base	394	76	100	134	81
	%	%	%	%	%
Tape films	46	40	54	45	43
Tape other programmes	61	77	63	54	57
Hire films	45	43	43	46	50
Too much rubbish on TV	13	11	9	13	19

(Multiple choice: columns add up to more than 100 per cent.)

suggests that there were an untapped set of desires in large sections of the British public which video partially satisfied – if nothing else it demonstrated the abiding love which the British have for films. There are two main reasons for acquiring a VCR: time-shifting and videotape rental, both of which revolve around the feature film.

Unsatisfied demand for a VCR was also unequally distributed: three-quarters of 16–29-year-olds wanted one compared to just over half of the 30–49-year-olds and around a quarter of those 50 and over. This last group shows the least interest in film, which might go some way to explaining their lack of interest in a VCR, but of course those on a state pension have an extremely low income, which militates against buying or renting a machine.

Although cost is overwhelmingly given as the reason for not acquiring a video, we know that cost is relative to the benefits which someone receives from the goods which they buy. Television sets are as expensive to rent or buy as VCRs, and yet virtually everyone has a television because it provides relaxation, information and entertainment. Even if poverty militates against owning a VCR among those on a subsistence income, money cannot be the main problem for the middle class or those with money to spend on leisure. One clue as to the difference between those who have video and those who do not lies in their attitude to broadcast television. Slightly less than two-thirds of those who have video claimed that recording other programmes was a reason for acquiring a VCR, while less than half of those without a VCR gave this as a reason for wanting one. People's attitudes to broadcast television and to feature films condition their reasons for wanting a VRC. If they want to choose the film or television programme which they are going to watch then they will buy a video. If, on the other hand, they are not concerned with choice, or if they think that they have sufficient choice, then the VCR recedes in importance.

TABLE 30

Reasons for wanting video

N = 276

	Total	AB	C1	C2	DE
Weighted Base	276	35	91	60	90
	%	%	%	%	%
Tape films	48	47	56	42	45
Tape other programmes	48	61	54	44	41
Hire films	40	38	40	42	42
Too much rubbish on TV	17	11	17	14	22

Although renting feature films is normally given as the single most important reason for wanting a VCR, there is a gap between intention and action. Principally, people do not hire feature films with the degree of regularity which one would anticipate from reasons they give for acquiring a VCR. Less than half the owners of VCRs rent feature films, and a familiar pattern has been established whereby new owners of machines sample feature film rental – in some extreme cases going through several a day – but very quickly run out of films to watch. Very few people increase their level of rental after the initial burst of enthusiasm, which demonstrates that people do not watch films indiscriminately but insist on choice, quality and range in films as in everything else.

The middle classes show the largest disparity between intention and action. The reason is simple; video rental shops do not cater for 'middle-brow' tastes, therefore the effort which goes into renting a film is not commensurate with the pleasure which the film provides. The clear difference between the middle class and the other class groups replicates the cinema attendance patterns of the 1940s and 1950s.

TABLE 31

Main uses of VCR

N = 391

	Total	AB	C1	C2	DE
Weighted Base	394	76	100	134	81
	%	%	%	%	%
Tape films	45	37	50	48	44
Tape other programmes	53	63	53	49	48
Hire films	30	18	32	31	37

(Multiple choice: columns add up to more than 100 per cent.)

Video rental, because it is a mass phenomenon, reflects mass taste more clearly than modern cinema attendance.

The key to understanding why some people do not want to rent feature films even although they own a VCR, or indeed why they do not want a VCR in the first place, might lie with their attitude to broadcast television. We can see how complex this is by the attitude of those on a subsistence

TABLE 32

Changes in videogram rental since first acquired video recorder

N = 348

	Total	AB	C1	C2	DE
Weighted Base	348	63	87	126	72
	%	%	%	%	%
Rent more	8	12	9	5	9
Rent less	49	40	45	61	43
Same	33	43	31	28	37
Don't know	10	5	15	6	11

income. These people are more likely to think that there is too much 'rubbish' on television. This does not imply a commitment to high culture. In essence it means that they do not like a lot of what they see. However, it is entirely possible that 'too much rubbish' judged on one cultural scale could mean that there is not enough 'rubbish' as others would define the term. For example, lower income groups

TABLE 33

Favourite television programmes

N = 795

	Total	Class				Video	
		AB	C1	C2	DE	Yes	No
Weighted Base	795	128	219	215	231	270	525
	%	%	%	%	%	%	%
Soap operas	29	22	28	32	33	29	30
Situation comedies	29	30	29	34	24	31	28
Other comedy programmes	16	19	14	18	16	18	15
Variety shows	9	1	10	7	15	4	12
Quiz shows	25	15	19	27	36	25	26
Sports	28	28	22	28	32	28	27
News	15	23	25	6	8	9	17
Wildlife programmes	39	31	37	45	38	38	39
Documentaries	32	50	30	34	21	33	31
Feature films	42	36	47	42	39	49	38
Game shows	8	4	5	6	15	8	8
Chat shows	10	16	10	6	11	11	10
Travel programmes	12	19	15	8	9	8	14
Religious programmes	1	2	*	—	—	*	1
Other	2	3	2	2	1	3	1
Don't know/no answer	1	—	1	1	—	1	*

* = less than 0.5

rated quizzes and game shows as the programmes they liked the most; therefore 'too much rubbish' is double-edged: it could refer either to documentaries (in the case of the working class) or quiz shows (in the case of the middle class). Either way the subjective judgement has objective consequences, because these people are less likely to want a VCR. One interesting afterthought about time-shifting films is that the favourite programmes of the owners of VCRs are feature films, whereas those not owning a video recorder prefer other types of television.

It is possible that people may exaggerate their preference for 'quality' programmes; the middle class in particular possess a self-identity of elite cultural attainment. Even though the middle classes may enjoy soap operas more than they are willing to admit, the differences between them and the working class are strong enough to suggest genuine dissimilarities of taste. From our point of view the interesting thing is that although taping feature films tops the middle-class list, it is an also-ran among the lower working class. For the latter films cannot compete with the pleasure gained

TABLE 34

Attitudes to amount of films on television

N = 795

	Total	16–29	30–49	50+	AB	C1	C2	DE
Weighted Base	795	227	346	210	128	219	215	231
	%	%	%	%	%	%	%	%
Too many	7	4	5	12	8	7	10	4
Too few	40	49	38	33	24	38	37	53
About right	50	45	52	52	67	51	50	39
Don't know	3	2	5	3	1	5	3	4
Total	100	100	100	100	100	100	100	100

from soap operas and the peculiar excitements of quiz shows like *The Price is Right*.

Notwithstanding these differences in taste, and despite the large numbers of feature films on television each week, most people want more films to be shown.

That films are 'on tap' has not detracted from their popularity. Persistent demands from all sections of the population for more films on television and for a wider range of films in video stores presents a picture of an insatiable audience, which, although critical of individual films, will watch what is dished up and evaluate films more highly than most other programmes.

This level of satisfaction with films is intriguing. It suggests that the frequency of visits to the cinema was accounted for by *films* in general rather than the *individual film*. The popularity of the cinema flowed not so much from any claim that this was the best place to watch films, but from the fact that it was the only place. The present levels of consumption of film – higher than it ever was during the most popular period of the cinema – is evidence only for a changed relationship to the cinema but not to film as such. Viewed this way, once cinema was in competition with its own product it was bound to lose.

We can see evidence for this in the relationship between the VCR and television. Although the ratings for broadcast television programmes drop a little as a result of people watching video, there is no evidence of a major shift away from television. Indeed, 12 per cent of our sample claimed their television viewing had actually increased as a result of owning a VCR. But for the overwhelming majority the possession of a VCR made no difference to the time spent watching television.

This commitment to broadcast television is partly a function of the ways that leisure is managed in the home. Established routines within the home, especially if shared with others, have special properties because they function as the management of the ways in which people live together. They become associated with feelings about correct behaviour and, in extremes cases, they prescribe appropriate behaviour, which if challenged undermines feelings of family or household solidarity. It is not surprising therefore that something as regular as watching television should not change with the introduction of video. The very regularity of viewing serves to regulate domestic life and hence cannot easily be altered without resulting in friction.

Routines which become part of the daily cycle of work and leisure lead to a feeling that life would be unimaginable without them. They become almost part of the natural world, like sleeping. The urgent call to the repair man when the television breaks down is not just the product of worries about missing certain programmes, but rather is related to the feeling that there is something lacking from the caller's life. The breakdown of the television set means the collapse of a routine which focuses someone's leisure and organises their time. This is an extremely unpleasant experience for most people, and leads to an urgent desire for normal service to be resumed as soon as possible.

Despite the routine nature of television watching, many people make a special effort to watch a feature film on television. It may be easier to watch a film at home, but nevertheless arrangements have to be made: for example, putting the children to bed; breaking meal-time habits by eating at different times or whilst watching the film; cutting short other activities to make certain one is home.

People's relationship to television is not a function of their general level of activity, i.e. if someone has regular out-of-home activities they are not more likely to make a special effort to watch a particular film than those who did not. Whether or not one is purposive in leisure terms and takes an active interest in pursuing leisure out of the home does not influence the amount of effort put into watching a film.

Thus, whilst films may be one of the most popular forms

TABLE 35

Make special effort to watch film on television

N = 795

	Total	16–29	30–49	50+	AB	C1	C2	DE
Weighted Base	795	227	346	210	128	219	215	231
	%	%	%	%	%	%	%	%
Yes- always	29	33	25	33	20	30	24	38
Yes- usually	28	27	28	34	29	27	26	27
Sometimes	32	33	38	20	31	31	37	30
No, never	9	7	8	14	12	8	12	5
Don't know	1	1	2	1	2	2	1	*

TABLE 36

Make special effort to watch films on television

		Outdoor Leisure (e.g. playing or watching sport, membership of voluntary associations)	
	Total	Yes	No
	%	%	%
Regularly	29	28	29
Usually	28	28	29
Sometimes	32	33	32
Never	9	9	9
Don't know/no answer	1	2	1

of entertainment on television their popularity cannot be separated from the popularity of television itself. Part of the reason why people will make a special effort to watch a film on television is that they enjoy being at home – the effort does not disrupt their lives in the way that out-of-home leisure does. The increasing comfort of homes has led to the popularity of watching films in the home, but because it provides entertainment television has increased the popularity of the home as a place in which to spend time.

3 How to Watch a Video

People do not try to recreate the viewing environment of the cinema when watching a film at home. For example, only 11 per cent turn off the lights when watching a rented video, and only 2 per cent take the phone off the hook. The overwhelming majority of people do not find it necessary to cut themselves off from their environment. The film is firmly placed within the context of the home, and nothing else need be added to the setting. For example, whereas 26 per cent of cinema-goers usually have a take-away meal before or after attending the cinema, only 6 per cent did so when renting a video. This suggests that even if renting a video is special, it is accommodated into everyday home-life. (Although 36 per cent had a drink while watching, this is probably a reflection of normal drinking habits.)

There is a striking similarity in the way that people watch films on television and on VCR, and this provides more support for the idea that video is television with a difference, rather than a corrupt form of cinema.

Other conclusions can also be drawn from these tables. For example, films are enjoyed so much that the conditions under which they are shown are to a large extent immaterial. Despite the physical limits of the television screen it is considered a perfectly good way of seeing a film. Why should it be otherwise? There is nothing about film as such that intrinsically demands a large screen; that was no more than a function of the history of film viewing – the marriage of social process and technology. In the long-term history of 'film' the cinema will come to be seen as a relatively transient

TABLE 37

Other things done when renting a film

N = 348

	Total	AB	C1	C2	DE
Weighted Base	348	63	87	126	72
	%	%	%	%	%
Make sure children in bed	19	23	24	14	21
Get take-away meal	6	12	2	5	6
Take the phone off the hook	2	—	2	2	2
Invite friends round	10	13	11	10	7
Turn off the lights	11	2	18	8	15
Have a drink	36	51	34	35	27
None of these	33	33	32	33	32
Don't know/no answer	7	3	8	7	9

TABLE 38

Things done while watching film on television

N = 795

	Total
	%
Have a drink	38
Get a take-away meal	5
Invite friends around	3
Make sure the children are in bed	17
Turn off the lights	11
Take the phone off the hook	1
None of these	40
Don't know/no answer	1

condition that was utterly changed by shifts in the social process and technology. Most of our evidence shows that individuals simply alter the ways in which they want to watch films, with none of the angst that so besets those for whom cinema is more important than film.

The fact that a feature film is 'meant' for something larger than a television screen is irrelevant to how it is viewed. People do not expect Cinerama on a 16-inch screen and are not disappointed with what they see. If this were not the case, and individuals constantly regretted they were not seeing the film as it was intended, it would be difficult to explain the high level of satisfaction with television as a medium for watching films. What we must understood, therefore, is not film and its properties but people and their propensities.

4   The Weekend Starts Here

The proposition that watching films on video fits the structure of people's lives is demonstrated by the fact that Saturday and Sunday are the two most popular days for watching video (though 59 per cent declared that they had no favourite).

While the availability of free time, a rise in disposable incomes and an absence of other leisure opportunities made cinema attendance not just possible but likely, the extension of free time and the increase in entertainment outlets worked against the cinema in favour of viewing film at home. Television did not drag the audience away but rather allowed an activity more in keeping with the changed circumstances of individual lives to develop.

The success story of television is as much social as it is technological. The cost of overlooking this point is to displace people as the focus of understanding cultural interaction and to transform them into mere constructs of entertainment technology, where they exist only as viewers and

TABLE 39

Day preferred for watching films

N = 348

	Total
	%
Monday	3
Tuesday	2
Wednesday	2
Thursday	2
Friday	6
Saturday	25
Sunday	15
No particular day	59
Don't know/no answer	–

TABLE 40A

Why certain days are preferred

N = 143

	Total
	%
No work that day/evening/no school	14
Do not have to get up next morning	5
Not much on TV	30
Only time at home/don't go out that evening	14
Family are all together/we all watch	9
Can keep videotape over weekend	10
Nothing else to do/clear day	6
Start of the weekend	6
More time to view	21
Other answers	5
Don't know/no answer	1

listeners, rather than real people who exist in other capacities outside their role as an audience. All entertainment – even slot machines – relates to the meanings of the rest of one's life. Few social workers would wish to be seen as the habitués of entertainment arcades, or even wish to pull the levers of slot machines. Their definition of self militates against the enjoyment of lining up symbols to win money, and against evaluating the playing of slot machines as a worthwhile activity. It could be expected from their work – which mixes observation, critical reflection and moral judgement – that their preferred form of entertainment would involve elements of personal control rather than chance. The greater the investment of personality the less likely that work and non-work are seen as separate.

By analysing the meaning of work for individuals it becomes easier to understand what type of entertainment they want. The 'back to work on Monday' mentality traditionally associated with the urban working class gives rise to the frenzied fun of Friday and Saturday night. However, Friday and Saturday night take on special significance only by comparison to the rest of the week. They lose their attraction as special times for fun if the rest of the week loses it grimness. Furthermore, they no longer operate as the relief from a world of drudgery that comes around all too quickly on Monday.

Leisure time is no longer so marked by the sight of crowds of people seeking relief from the working week. The decline of the queue as a common social phenomenon, be it the queue for the public house, the football match or the cinema, is in part the result of the extension of leisure and softening of work which has left the individual with greater responsibility for how they will organise free time. There is no need for entertainment to be crammed into a specific time slot and psychologically there is less need to justify having a good time. Activities that were once enthusiastically engaged in because they were the accepted notion of what leisure consisted of are increasingly being questioned as the nature of work changes.

However, monotony and the tedium of routine are still characteristics of much modern work. Those with monotonous jobs continue to *long* for the weekend. Watching a video has become part of the weekend for people with monotonous and boring jobs; renting a film is now almost as important as going out for a drink on a Saturday night.

TABLE 40B

Longing for the weekend

| | Total | Monotonous Work | | Prefer | | |
		Agree	Disagree	Cinema	Video	TV
Weighted Base	410	86	289	144	102	143
I often find myself longing for the weekend						
	%	%	%	%	%	%
Agree strongly	9	23	6	8	14	9
Agree	38	54	33	30	44	41
Neither	10	2	12	12	3	12
Disagree	37	21	43	47	33	32
Disagree strongly	3	1	5	3	5	3
Don't know/no answer	2	–	1	1	1	3

(Base does not add up due to sub-sampling variation.)

In this section we have shown that watching films on VCRs and on television is a different but not inferior experience from doing so at the cinema. People have special ways of, and special days for, watching films on all three media, and they choose the one which best fits their needs. This raises the question of cost. Are people choosing to watch on television simply because they cannot afford to do so at the cinema,

or do they consider television and video to be better forms
of entertainment?

5   The Cost of Control

Those who possess a VCR are more likely to consider the
cinema as bad value for money compared to other entertainments than those without a video.

TABLE 41

Value of cinema compared to other entertainments

N = 388

(All who had been to cinema in last year)

	Total	Age			Class					Video	
		16–29	30–39	40+	AB	C1	C2	DE		Yes	No
Weighted Base	388	186	118	84	86	117	101	84		162	226
	%	%	%	%	%	%	%	%		%	%
Good	50	46	56	49	60	49	49	43		45	53
Bad	29	32	25	28	17	29	29	43		35	25
Same	18	20	16	17	18	21	19	12		18	18
Don't know/ no answer	3	2	3	5	5	2	3	2		2	4

Even amongst fairly regular attenders (four times a year
or more) one-quarter considered the cinema bad value. Only
4 per cent of those who ever rented video thought they were
bad value compared to other forms of entertainment.

Income partly determines whether someone thinks of video
rental as good value for money. For example, more than

TABLE 42

Value of video films compared to other forms of entertainment

N = 348 (All who ever rent video films)

	Total	AB	C1	C2	DE
Weighted Base	348	63	87	126	72
	%	%	%	%	%
Good	84	92	83	85	79
Bad	4	1	5	5	6
About the same	4	3	3	4	6
Don't know/no answer	7	4	9	6	10

two-fifths of DEs regard the cinema as bad value, compared to less than one-fifth of DEs. One might have expected the very cheapness of video to be seen as better value by the DEs than the wealthier ABs. After all, the most common cost of renting a video in 1984 was only £1, and it is difficult to imagine what other form of entertainment could be had at such a low cost. People on lower incomes are far heavier renters than those in professional and managerial occupations; roughly half of the former hire between one and three films a week compared to only one-quarter of the latter. Renting is so cheap that if one could not afford to do so, it is doubtful one could afford to buy or rent a VCR in the first place. However, there is a difference between something being good value, and buying it because it is good value. Fashion clothes, for example, are not always good value in terms of the cost or quality of material. Their purchase depends rather upon questions of style and self-image.

How far the comparative price of video enters as a factor in judging the cost of a visit to the cinema is difficult to say. Although 42 per cent of video-owners said that they did not go to the cinema more often because it was too expensive, this is no different from non-video-owners, 38 per cent of whom also claimed that cost influences their lack of cinema attendance. However, as one quarter of those who had a VCR in their homes claimed that they attended the cinema less often as a result, we cannot completely write off the video effect. It may be the video recorder is an obvious rather than the real reason for attendance declining. Nevertheless, 35 per cent claimed they did in fact go less frequently once they had a video, with 60 per cent claiming that it made no difference. In fact, the latter are closer to the truth than they could possibly realise. Cinema-going is such a low frequency activity that it is virtually impossible to point to any specific activity which would influence attendance. For example, practically three-quarters of those who claimed that they attended the cinema less frequently as a result of having a VCR had not set foot in a cinema in the previous year.

Yet whatever the actual basis for not doing something, the reasons given are important in understanding how activities are viewed, and it is interesting that whilst 13 per cent of those without video gave 'Not interested/don't care for films' as a reason for non-attendance, only 5 per cent of those with video did. This is consistent with the reasons for obtaining a video in the first place. It may seem an obvious point that it is interest in film that is related to cinema-going, but it is also the case that interest in film was the determining factor in getting a video. Not surprisingly therefore video owners go to the cinema more frequently than non-owners.

It is in this context that we need to examine the evidence on the relative price of cinema and video. Objectively the cost of the cinema ticket may not be expensive compared to the price of a pint of beer, but going to the cinema is, when it includes other forms of entertainment. People rationalise their preference for video over cinema by comparing the prices which they have to pay for one or the other. Most feel that the experience of watching the film is the same regardless of the setting and that the comparative expense of the cinema ticket compares unfavourably with renting a video. But price is not really the issue. If cinema tickets cost the same as renting a video, cinema attendances would not shoot up to the same level as video rentals. The cinema will never see 300 million attendances again, regardless of ticket prices.

Conclusion

The accretion of respectability to forms of entertainment is intriguing: rugby union is more respectable than rugby league, cricket more so than football. Whether a pastime is acceptable or not owes much to the status of the participants; for example, fox hunting would be considered a coarse and degrading activity if pursued by the working classes. The history of audiovisual entertainment reflects the class-based nature of respectable entertainment. It was the cinema's massive popularity among the urban working classes that prevented it from securing outright moral approval. In particular, religious and educational groups considered the cinema to be a distracting pursuit which threatened more worthwhile activities. As cinema has declined as a mass enter-tainment and become an art form these same groups now regret cinema's disappearance. Television has come along to soak up the excess disapproval. The guardians of moral and intellectual culture regard it as a mindless activity, and it is blamed for a variety of social ills. Television and video take the heat and cinema-going has become a respectable activity.

This chapter has argued that watching film on television or video should not be looked down upon as some massively inferior experience. The majority of the population prefer to watch films at home and have good reasons, rooted in the fabric of their lives, for so doing. Thus far in this book we have explored film in the context of people's lives, focusing on the social structure and social experience. But there comes a point when we must turn to the question of what it is about films which separates them from other forms of audiovisual entertainment and other types of leisure. In short, we must address the question of taste. It is to this complex issue that we now turn.

CHAPTER 4

The Pleasures of Films

WHY DO ex-grammar school boys quote large chunks of *Monty Python and the Holy Grail* and young British blacks join Kung Fu clubs after seeing Bruce Lee films? Whatever happened to Westerns? Why will over 100 million people see *Rocky V*? Why do some people think that a black and white film with subtitles is the most boring thing on earth whilst for others it is the definition of paradise? The answers to these questions require us to enter the murky waters of taste and sensibility. We need to look at the needs and desires films fulfil and the pleasures films bring.

On the surface people go to films for the same reason as they always did. Primarily, people say, the story is the most important element in choosing a film. This was true in 1946, when four out of ten in a *News Chronicle* survey claimed that the story was the most important factor guiding their choice of film, and remains true today, when around half claim that the story is the most important element.

Not only has the reason for seeing a film not changed substantially down the years, the type of film which people want to see has remained roughly stable. Although Westerns, war and science fiction films have changed places in the order of preference, comedy remains king.

These types of surveys can merely scratch the surface of pleasure and taste. It is important to dig deeper if we are to answer more fundamental questions about the social roots

TABLE 43

Factors guiding the audience in its choice

	%
The story	37
Who is in it	34
Reviewer's opinions	19
The title	16
The cinema	9
Friend's recommendations	2
It's British	1

Source: News Chronicle

TABLE 44

Most important reason for seeing film

N = 795

	Total	Age 16–29	30–49	50+	Single Steady	Single Not Steady	Married
Weighted Base	795	227	346	210	73	74	556
	%	%	%	%	%	%	%
Plot/storyline	49	54	49	44	46	39	53
Type of film	24	24	30	14	35	27	24
Acting/stars	17	14	14	24	11	26	16
Music	3	2	2	5	2	1	2
Setting/scenery	3	*	3	8	*	4	3
Special effects	3	6	3	1	4	9	2
Director	1	*	2	*	1	2	1

TABLE 45

Preferences for types of films amongst persons of different age groups: 1965

N = 2,000

	Age			
	16–19	20–29	30–49	50 and over
Usually enjoy:	%	%	%	%
Comedies	79	77	78	68
Films with serious story	53	66	75	75
Crime and thriller	58	56	52	41
Historical	29	38	45	50
Musicals	45	54	43	38
War films	45	33	29	18
Epics	50	23	26	24
Westerns	16	25	20	10
Avant-garde	3	25	18	14
Science fiction	29	13	12	9
Horror films	24	3	7	2

(Source: BBC Audience Research Department)

of pleasure and the relationship between pleasure and behaviour. Ever since the Lumière brothers produced the first fiction film psychologists, educationalists, priests, sociologists, the Hayes Committee, the British Board of Film Censors, Mary Whitehouse, newspapers and critics have asked 'why do people like this?' and 'what harm is it doing to them?' In 1985 the Conservative Government supported Graham Bright's Private Member's bill for censoring video films and for applying stricter criteria for videos than for films released in the cinema. Prior to the introduction of the Bill the media had worked itself up into a frenzy over video nasties, producing improbable statistics showing that two out of every three children had seen one.

TABLE 46

Three favourite types of films: 1984

N = 795

		Age		
	Total	16–29	30–49	50+
Weighted Base	795	227	346	210
	%	%	%	%
Comedy	19	23	18	17
Science fiction	7	11	8	2
Horror	6	14	5	1
War	7	5	7	8
Adult films	1	3	1	1
Western	6	3	7	7
Thriller	15	13	17	15
Romance	9	9	8	9
Drama	9	5	10	14
Adventure	10	9	11	10
Musical	8	5	6	13
Other	2	2	1	2
Don't know	1	*	*	2

(Source: Broadcasting Research Unit)

The assumption behind the Bright Bill and the prevailing moral panic was that films had the power to corrupt. This is not a new idea. In the United States in the 1930s the Payne Foundation commissioned reports on the effects of feature films on children. Their answer was that films could not create racism, violence, or criminality, but if such social and psychological conditions existed then films could help to confirm them. In the 1950s and 1960s the moral panic about the effects of audiovisual material switched from cinema to television and the arguments made in the Payne Foundation studies were resurrected in television studies.

Rather than rake over all these arguments again, we decided to look not at the effects of films but instead focus on more general questions of taste and pleasure. In his book *The Pleasure of the Text* Roland Barthes argued: 'No sooner has a word been said, somewhere, about the pleasure of the text, than two policemen are ready to jump on you: the political policeman and the psychoanalytical policeman: futility and/or guilt, pleasure is either idle or vain, a class notion or an illusion'. Sometimes sociologists feel like the policemen of pleasure – the Sweeney of the text. When we approach the question of pleasure we can only do so through *social* experience. We recognise that pleasure is not limited to its social dimensions but our study concentrates on the topography of pleasure, leaving the aesthetic and psychoanalytic dimensions to others.

1   Who put the 'Mass' in Mass Media?

Before World War II many social commentators acted as pleasure policemen; in particular they were not at all keen on pleasure gained through the mass media (see Perlman 1936). Preoccupied with the problem of mass society, many felt that urbanisation, industrialisation and the mass media had undermined the cultural diversity and heterogeneity of the myriad of small geographic and ethnic groups which made up the American melting pot. The one-dimensional view of the audience encapsulated in mass society theory viewed the cinema as the product of, and contributor to, 'massification' (*sic*). As small communities dissolved into mass society the institutional frameworks for establishing individual identity no longer existed. As a result the urban mass turned to the cinema and the mass media, which expressed the alienated and alienating values of industrialism.

This position was held by cultural elitists on all sides of the political spectrum. Paul Rosenberg spoke of the mass media promoting tyranny in the cultural realm, and in his usual high-handed fashion Theodor Adorno claimed that the power of the culture industry's ideology was such that conformity had replaced consciousness. According to this perspective the mass media dealt in lowest common denominator junk. Films for the masses were without value: lots of action, guns, cars, wealth, sex and jokes without any redeeming feature.

Fundamentally, mass society theorists and cultural critics thought that taste and pleasure were simply the products of bureaucratic and industrial monotony. Although understandable as a response to fascism, the development of impersonal interaction, and the industrialisation of the distribution and reception of images and messages, it could ultimately be seen as elitist. As the post-war period wore on and vigorous popular cultures emerged, mass society theory was progressively undermined, aided, it should be added, by empirical research in the new discipline of communications studies. The dominant view now is that audiences cannot be treated as a uniform mass and that message reception is not a unidimensional process. Mass audiences are now regarded, in a non-derogatory manner, as aggregates of people making similar choices but who are too many to have any face to face interaction. (see Escarpit 1977)

The rejection of elitist views of popular culture was pioneered in the UK by Richard Hoggart in *The Uses of Literacy* and Raymond Williams in *Communications*. Although these commentators had many fundamental disagreements they consistently argued that working-class taste and pleasure should not be treated as second-rate or worn-out culture.

The call for an analysis of the diversity of response to mass media messages has not been the sole preserve of communications researchers. The anthropologists Mary Douglas and Pierre Bourdieu have both done significant work in this area. (Bourdieu 1985, Douglas and Isherwood 1979; see also Garnham and Williams 1980) Bourdieu argues that taste is a function of the relationship of the individual to financial and cultural capital. If someone has considerable financial wealth they do not need education to achieve power or status. The social mobility of those without such financial wealth is in the main determined by education, and as education structures taste there will be many differences between those with cultural capital and those without.

Douglas argues that taste is a function of the experience of group identity and social hierarchy. She suggests that audience research must be able to account for the fact that specific messages 'reach right through the class structure'. Her own proposal is that vertical taste groups exist which cut through class and demonstrate the similarities in taste between top bureaucrats and those who work at the Post Office counter.

Douglas and Wollaeger have a fourfold typology of the relation between taste and identity (see over). The *grid* refers to social constraints imposed by beliefs, values, norms, etc, and *group* to social constraints based on the intensity and nature of social interaction. They argue that, 'The interaction of these two dimensions defines four social contexts in which different patterns of rewards and penalties and their moral justification arise.' For instance, the mass of the industrial working class are contrained by rules made by others. They are insulated from collective experience and have little sense of making their own world (Social Experience 1 in the following diagram). These individuals prefer dramas or stories set against a recognisable background in which the characters understand and accept their social position. Essentially, they want the fictional world to be dominated by rule-governed behaviour, e.g. police and hospital dramas, although in the fantasy variant roles are reversed; police become criminals (*Serpico*) and secretaries dominate their boss (*9 to 5*). The drama is the outgrowth of the performance of social rules, and the personal characteristics of the characters are secondary to the story. Violence is an effective means of maintaining order but it is seldom highlighted for its own sake.

A Typology of Public Viewing	
GRID	
+	
1: Insulated individuals	2: Hierarchical groups
Social Experience Individualist but constrained by rules made by others	*Social Experience* Collectivist/Hierarchic
Aesthetic Preference Routinised situations Dramas of reconciliation	*Aesthetic Preference* Dramas of social harmony
GROUP	
− +	
3: Enterprising individuals	4: Egalitarian groups
Social Experience Individualist/Competitive Entrepreneurial	*Social Experience* Collectivist, small group covert internal opposition
Aesthetic Preferences Dramas of individual quest	*Aesthetic Preferences* Dramas of disruption
(Adapted from Douglas and Wollaeger 1984)	

Other social experiences are highly individualistic but the individuals are in relative control of their lives and the rules and culture by which they live (Social Experience 3). This is true of entrepreneurs, artists, film directors, or any freelance occupation where individualism predominates and authority is seen as an obstruction. These people are attracted by stories concerning individual achievement and success. More often than not the enemy turns out to be a major corporation or a large-scale bureaucratic organisation. If film directors are included in this group, the question arises: has the move from factory-style to freelance production meant that directors produce culturally ambiguous films with which those in mundane or routine jobs do not identify? Part of the success of Hollywood might have been that factory-style production created working conditions for the producers of films which led to a natural affinity with the audience. This question is well beyond the remit of this book but would certainly repay investigation.

Third come people who work for large organisations which are collectivist and hierarchical (Social Experience 2), demanding a high degree of loyalty and commitment. Because people who work in this environment are sure of the rules they live by (reinforced by their group loyalty), they are freer than individualists to reflect on the ordered world in which they find themselves. They prefer films and television programmes which focus on rites of passage, births, deaths, marriages — in effect the persistence and continuity of the group. Stories about social groups which are well regulated and ordered, where conflict and debate are undermined by appearing ludicrous, also appeal.

The final group comprises those whose experience is collective and egalitarian (4). Because they have powerful commitments to one another they have to rationalise conflict as something which is supernatural, and which appears from outside the group. Because the boundaries between insider and outsider are constantly being reinforced in these supernatural dramas, the unnatural is a commonplace leitmotif; both humans and nature are capable of turning nasty in unexpected ways. Youth peer groups, with their strong internal loyalties and sense of boundaries, are likely to have preferences which reflect the taste for the world turning nasty. This goes some way to explaining their taste for horror films of the *Friday the 13th* variety. We will follow up the relationship between youth and horror films throughout this chapter as it provides us with an interesting way to explore the relationship between social experience and film taste.

Although the Douglas and Wollaeger typology attempts to escape from simplistic horizontal class analysis it is somewhat schematic and theoretical. Empirical research which explores the differences within socio-economic groups has been limited. One interesting study conducted by Deanna Robinson looked at differences in taste and pleasure within an upper middle-income group. Robinson pointed out that teachers, lecturers and those concerned with education in general were more committed to film than professionals such as lawyers and doctors. She also pointed out that those who were 'housewives', in a traditional sense, had a different attitude to film from women who were employed. Although all of the housewives in Robinson's small study had been teachers they shared a non-analytical approach toward television and film. They were infrequent cinema attenders and prefered films such as *Summer of '42*, i.e. romantic fiction. (Robinson 1975) Whilst Robinson's study is illuminating it was based on only a small sample, and, like Douglas, it does not explore the nature of fantasy, the projection of the self into characters and plots which are the opposite of one's social experience. People may actually reject their work experience in their leisure pursuit.

Much of the literature on cinema assumes that it is a dream factory, a place for play and exploration, where for the space of two hours the employees of a large-scale bureaucracy can be entrepreneurs, and escape the feeling that their lives are bound up with the impersonal rules of the hierarchy. As they walk out of the door of the cinema they may say 'what a lot of nonsense', but for the duration of the film they want to be Han Solo, Dirty Harry, Rocky or Calamity Jane. They know it is not part of the 'real' world, but they value the fantasy.

By and large individuals feel some kind of loose emotional affinity with characters in a film. But for some people films spill out into their everyday lives. This can lead to an imitation of the behavioural and physical characteristics of a star, for example doing Clint Eastwood's walk or having a hairstyle like Joan Collins. In some extreme cases people may change their politics, religion, or sexuality in favour of those practised by their favourite star. There is a continuum from the simple imitation of a character to the introjection of that character's behaviour or the projection of one's own fantasies onto a star or character. Most people stay at the low end of the continuum. (Tudor 1974)

According to our survey the most common reason for selecting a film star as favourite is that they are a good actor, followed by the identification between a star and a certain type of film. At a conscious level at least people do not like a star because they are macho or masculine (5%), have personality or charisma (4%) or sex appeal (1%), and even less because they 'would like to be like him/her' (less than 1%). Most people describe stars as always giving a good performance (45%), picking good roles (19%) or having screen presence (20%). Physical characteristics such as handsomeness (10%) or sexual attractiveness (13%) come much further down the list. The relation between the life experience of the individual and the story or stars with which they identify must be related to the question of fantasy. Although, on the whole, people identify most strongly with characters of their sex, age and class, stars can transcend this and unite disparate groupings in a common pleasure. (Dyer 1979)

As we noted in the introduction, psychologists have spent a great deal of time on this problem, but, without detracting from their research, the simple fact is that films represent both the world as people experience it *and* a space outside the everyday in which people can indulge in fantasies which have no bearing on the experience of the real world. Our research demonstrates that individuals move along the fantasy continuum depending on their stage in the lifecycle. There are close connections between the social structure of leisure and taste which cannot be ignored.

2 Nights Out and Video Nasties: Film Taste and Film Culture

Surveys are rather blunt instruments in the areas of taste and sensibility. So in order to flesh out attitudes to film we decided to use discussion groups. First of all we convened a preliminary discussion group, recruited from people recommended by friends (the friends not being included in the group, for obvious reasons). On the basis of statements made during this initial discussion we developed the attitude questionnaire, which had 109 statements, with a five-point scale from completely agree to completely disagree (see Appendix). This questionnaire was then administered to ten discussion groups, each of which contained between eight and ten people. We then analysed the answers and produced several sets of attitudes which exposed the range of opinions and views about films and the cinema. This statistical analysis is interesting and valuable, but the real richness, as we shall see later, comes from the discussions themselves, which throw up a range of contradictory views which the statistical analysis did not expose.

First, we shall look at the relationship between work and film taste which most researchers assume as a background to their thinking about the film audience. We explored this by administering two further questionnaires about work and family experience, which we then correlated with the attitude statements about film. Below is a list of summarised attitudes to films, derived solely from the attitude questionnaire administered to the discussion groups. Several statements hang together (as revealed by the factor analysis), but some individual statements sum up the cluster of statements. The first cluster of statements given below (Pure Entertainment) is the one most generally held in the population. The others are given in descending order of universality:

1. Pure Entertainment
'It adds to the enjoyment of a film if it is set in a luxurious place.' 'A good film has good special effects.'
2. Video Valuing
'Because of the video, I have a greater interest in films.' 'I do not like TV films as much now that I have a video.'
3. Identification
'Watching people with problems puts my own into perspective.' 'Films provide insights into my own problems.'
4. Social Watching
'I enjoy watching video films with friends.' 'I don't like going to the cinema on my own.'
5. Individualist/Anti-Consensus
'I like films where violent forces take hold of people and disrupt their lives.' 'I like to see a rebel who gets away with things.'
6. Family togetherness
'I like the fact that we spend more time together now that we have a video.' 'We watch more films together now that we have a video.'
7. Message Receiver
'The films I enjoy most are when individuals struggle against adversity to achieve something.' 'The films I enjoy the most try to make a point.'
8. Video Escapism
'I really look forward to hiring a video.' 'Films about ordinary people and ordinary events are boring.'

9. Video Lovers

'I prefer to hire videos at weekends.' 'Now that I have a video I see less of my friends.'

These clusters of attitudes (or factors) indicate that there are three groups of reasons for watching films: content, identification, and social interaction. Factor 1, which is solely concerned with entertainment, is the one most generally held: most people take pleasure in films which are fast-moving, have good special effects, and do not challenge or threaten them in any way.

Four factors deal in various ways with identification. Those who hold the attitudes expressed in Factor 3 see films as a rehearsal of problems which they might confront, and an exploration of ways of dealing with these problems. Although films are important in this respect people will rarely identify with solutions which are clearly opposed to their own values. A liberal-minded student will not turn into a vigilante after watching *Death Wish*.

Factors 5, 7 and 8 express different facets of the pleasure of identification: 5 is about overturning authority, whereas 7 is concerned with struggling against the odds rather than against the system; 8 expresses traditional attitudes that films should enable the viewer to escape the mundane into a more interesting and glamorous world. Factor 5 summarises the attitudes of the majority of young regular cinema-attenders. Interaction is clearly important as a reason for film use, as can be seen from Factor 4, in which friends are identified as being the main reason for attending the cinema, and Factor 6, in which family life is enhanced by video ownership. The distribution of taste is not random, as can be seen from its relation to work and the family.

The work factors are given in the same format as the film taste factors (some statements are given in a negative form (−) as they express strong disagreement with the factor):

1. Lack of interest in work
'I find my work dull and boring.' 'My work is interesting and satisfying.' (−)
2. Group experience
'I work on my own.' (−) 'It is more important to spend time with your family than to get on in the world.' 'My work is team work.'
3. Routine
'I would like my work if I was appreciated more.' 'There is too much routine in my work.'
4. Pressure of work
'I worry about my work a lot.' 'Difficult to relax and not think of work.'
5. Supervised daydreaming
'I am left alone to run my work as I think fit.' (−) 'My superior checks up on me.' 'I find myself thinking about film characters when I am at work.'
6. Pressurised daydreaming
'When working I daydream a lot.' 'It's easy to make mistakes in my work.'
7. Disenchanted escapism
'I don't know how people filled their time before TV.' 'I can't wait for Friday and the weekend.' 'Most characters in films are unrealistic.'
8. Satisfaction
'I think that I have a pleasant life.' 'I think that the people I work with are interesting.'

There are indications of a strong relationship between group identity and attitudes to film. People who have a strong sense of group identity (Work Factor 2) are not particularly interested in going to the cinema, whereas those who strongly identify with anti-consensual values are the most regular cinema-attenders.

This begins to confirm our idea that certain types of experience of the social world, which are relatively independent of class, are determinants of film taste. Lack of interest in work was related to social film watching; pressurised daydreaming was related to individualism and anti-consensus; disenchanted escapism was related to pure entertainment; those who expressed satisfaction with their occupation did not identify with films. Having said that, the actual connections between film taste and work is by no means direct, and there are traces of an alternative explanation.

Work experience and film taste are strongly related to age. Young people relate positively to anti-consensus values (Film Factor 5), and to daydreaming (Work Factor 6) and escapism (Work Factor 7). On the other hand young people feel isolated in their work experience and do not have a strong sense of group solidarity (Work Factor 2). The film taste of young people and their continued interest in the cinema is strongly related to a weak sense of community and group solidarity and the loosening of the ties which bind young individuals to their families and the wider social institutions. Those who live with their parents are less likely to be isolated from the wider culture than those in flat-shares, which explains why open households produce regular cinema-attenders who take great pleasure in the film and identify strongly with the characters.

Having a family or a steady relationship increases the sense of solidarity and cultural conservativeness. Films which express uncongenial values are left behind in the lifecycle at precisely the same time as the home becomes the focus for solidarity. Negative feelings about family, work or education are more important determinants of film taste and cinema attendance than occupation or income.

We decided to explore this more fully by putting the most representative attitude statements, drawn from the discussion groups, into the national survey. This confirmed that there are four basic elements to people's attitudes to film. Most people see films in terms of leisure: statistically, the most commonly held view was: 'Films must be part of an evening out for me to enjoy them.' Second, most people feel that films should not threaten their values or psychological security: statements like 'I can't enjoy films if they are very violent' and 'I don't like horror and adventure films which portray the world as a dangerous place' were commonly expressed. In other words, people want films to confirm safe consensual values. Third, some people go to films because they identify strongly with the characters or the story. This is expressed by statements such as: 'I daydream a lot about films and film characters', 'I sometimes try to behave like a character that I have seen in a film', and 'Films can make you feel discontented with life.' Finally, and simply, people like fast-moving, well-told stories: 'I don't like films with a complicated plot' is a classic expression of this attitude. These four – leisure, consensus, identification and narrative – form the framework for differences in film taste.

The ways in which these elements combine reveal a great deal about people's attitudes. Statistically, most people combine leisure with consensual attitudes. Social groups who have the most to gain from stability tend to want films to reflect a coherent and ordered world. Professionals, managers, married people, young people in a steady relationship and others who have a great deal invested in stable, functioning social systems do not want films to suggest that this stability is a chimera, or that it should be attacked and disrupted. But, interestingly, our discussion groups showed that unemployed people also seem more prone to these attitudes, which may suggest that they have enough trouble in their lives and want to see movies where everyone is secure in their position and has a recognisable function. The fact that the same film can act both as a extension of the social experience of the middle class and a fantasy for the unemployed means that we have to be extremely careful in generalising about the social organisation of pleasure.

Some people combine a high evaluation of cinema as a leisure activity with a strong interest in identifying with characters. Those who regularly pay to watch films are more likely to identify (in the most general sense) with characters, stars and plots. This attitude is more common among the young single working class than any other group, but if members of this group have a steady relationship, the level of identification is weaker and they are more likely to see films *simply* as leisure. They have less patience with complex stories and if they have to watch a complex film they want it to portray consensual values. This reflects the reasons for attending the cinema. If someone's primary reason for attending is to have a night out with a boyfriend or girlfriend they will not want to see morally or narratively ambiguous films which undermine social relationships. But even those who attend the cinema regularly and who identify most strongly with characters do not want the action slowed down to develop that characterisation. If the film is not pacy and slick this group are as likely to complain as any other.

The final group is committed to simple straightforward narrative films and is anti-consensual in their values. This group wants aggressive disruptive films with pacy stories, which Hollywood increasingly provides.

The social formation of these attitudes reveals that *on average* men are more prepared than women to tolerate complex plots, although this is complicated by a strong male tendency to like films which develop hell-for-leather regardless of characterisation. Women in our survey tended to see films simply as leisure, and to like films which express consensual values. The age breakdown reveals that 16- to 29-year-olds are much more likely to identify with films, value cinema more highly as a leisure habit, are able to handle more complex plots, and prefer films which are anti-authoritarian or at very least not unthinkingly consensual.

The class breakdown is interesting in the light of the arguments developed above about work and taste. Those in lower white-collar occupations are the most conservative film users and rank highest on the combination of leisure and consensus; the skilled and semi-skilled working class ranks highest on fast-paced, normatively disruptive films and lowest on the leisure/consensus couplet; the unskilled working class ranks highest on valuing cinema as a night out, but also strongly identifies with characters (suggesting that the old argument about the relationship between routine work and levels of identification has some validity); finally, professionals and management evaluate the cinema as more than simply a leisure pursuit (i.e. as having some intrinsic worth), but they do not identify strongly with characters. In other words, although they are committed to the cinema they keep their distance from the emotional and cognitive processes which facilitate identification.

Our research shows that pleasure *is* related to social experience, as Douglas and Wollaeger suggest, but that experience is mediated by family and courtship, rather than occupation on its own. This can be seen from an analysis of the film fantasies of young people, particularly those taking up jobs and acquiring new social responsibilities.

3 Rocky Horror and Adolescent Fantasy

'Go ahead, punk, make my day.' Whose fantasy is this? A middle-aged man telling young kids to shoot at him so he can blow their heads off smacks of consensual values of a particular kind; if you cannot get them to join you, blow them away. If it is consensual then it should appeal mainly to non-cinema-goers, but, in point of fact Mayor Clint Eastwood's *Sudden Impact* did pretty well in UK cinemas, coming eighth in the box office for 1984. Eastwood is perhaps a bad example in that the Harry Callaghan character in the Dirty Harry films and the Man with No Name spaghetti Westerns have framed his persona as a non-conformist avenger, but it is important to realise that you cannot simply read off the pleasure of the film from the values which it espouses. Values are clues to analysing pleasure but there can be little doubt that a story told by a master film-maker with major publicity back-up (such as *ET*) can cut across all the categories.

Although sociologists should be cautious about generalising from limited cases, on occasion we feel that a phenomenon comes along which completely confirms one's analysis. *The Rocky Horror Picture Show* is a paradigm case of middle-class youth fantasy, and repays detailed examination. The film, which starred Tim Curry, was based on a successful stage musical. Initially, it received bland reviews and low audiences, but at New York's Waverley Theatre in April 1976 a group of people turned up to a midnight screening dressed as some of the characters. As the cult developed the audience, many of whom had seen the film dozens of times, started to call out the dialogue and shots. During one scene, when a young couple are lost in the rain, it became customary to fire water pistols into the air and shine torches in order to help the couple. Interestingly, the cult was celebrated in Alan Parker's film *Fame*, where the young people in an acting school exhibited the full-blown characteristics of the cult.

Bruce Austin looked at a couple of *Rocky Horror* audiences three years after the cult began. He discovered that around two-thirds had seen the film more than once and that one person had seen it 200 times! The audience was made up of predominantly young (age 17–22), white (98.7%), college students (61.9%), who attended the film in mixed-sex groups of four or five. Over half of the audience took props to the film, including water pistols and rice for the wedding scene, and around one in ten dressed up as one of the characters. The latter were mainly people who had been to see the film regularly. Austin rightly argues that the film is part of an event which is composed of queuing for tickets, chatting to friends, chatting up strangers, participating in the film, and, to a certain extent, being part of something. (Austin 1981) Going to *Rocky Horror* is undoubtedly a celebration of all the elements of identification which we described above. It is adolescent collective consciousness writ large and as such is extremely unusual. Cinema attendance and film use among the general population, particularly among the British, involves a much less intense involvement with films, as the discussion groups which we conducted demonstrate.

4   Fear and Pleasure

Although films are quite far down in the list of possible pleasures there can be little doubt that people do enjoy them. The question is: is there a pattern to pleasure? The discussion groups provide rich evidence of a pattern along the lines of the family/individualist axis which we have been developing in this chapter.

Among the middle class, fear of social disruption played a part in enjoying certain films. In our commercial middle-class group people moved from approving of the police actions at Orgreave, which was the scene of a great deal of violence during the miners strike of 1984, to approving of Michael Winner's *Death Wish* films. One woman said of the police at Orgreave: 'hit first and ask later'; unsurprisingly she went on to say of Charles Bronson's *Death Wish* character: 'I could relate to that man.' Clearly there is a connection between general social and political attitudes and the level of identification with certain characters.

On the other hand, anything which is a threat to the smooth running of the social world disrupts pleasure. Even a threat to health is seen to be dangerous and militates against enjoying a film. Another commercial middle-class discussant claimed that she 'hated every moment' of *Silkwood*, in which the main character dies of radiation-induced cancer. She went on to say that the film left her feeling disturbed for 'at least half an hour afterwards'. Several important aspects of the relationship between taste and fear can be established here. First, *Silkwood* doubly threatened this woman; the physical threat of cancer was disturbing enough, but if it had been an act of God and the character had fought the cancer the film might have been acceptable (the noble death movie has been around almost as long as there have been feature films). But the cancer was the result of the character working in the nuclear industry, and her attempts to expose the connection between cancer and radiation led to attempts on her life from the industry, with the collusion of the government. The cancer was both physical and metaphorical and left the viewer feeling disturbed and unhappy. However, this feeling – even at this relatively extreme level – lasted only for half an hour. It may have had a longer-term unconscious effect on the woman but the film clearly did not affect her to any great degree. She was not entertained and though her world view was challenged, the foundations were not shaken.

The London working class were also very explicit as to what they did not like in films. For instance, one person claimed that *Gandhi* was the first film that he had walked out of, and indeed the whole group agreed: 'none of us could sit through *Gandhi*'. There might be racist undertones in this sentiment, but the reasons that they gave had more to do with the pace of the film and its quasi-cultural overtones than with the fact that Gandhi was an Indian. Another film which they hated was Al Pacino's *Cruising*, which was about a murder among the gay community in America. They were quite explicit that they did not like the film because it showed homosexual acts. The threat of 'deviant' sexual practices clashed with the conservativism of this group and regardless of the pace, camera work and narrative drive of *Cruising* this group did not like it.

The correlation between conservative taste and advancing age is fairly well established but, under certain circumstances, conservative tastes appear among the young. We conducted a discussion with police cadets in order to evaluate the strength of relationship between occupation and taste. Their favourite actors were Clint Eastwood, in the *Dirty Harry* films, and Charles Bronson in *Death Wish*. They were asked whether they thought it incongruous to identify with films in which ordinary policemen and women are shown to be stupid, corrupt and uncaring, and vigilante or non-conformist policemen clean up the streets using violence and fear. The cadets justified themselves by claiming that it was 'just fiction' and therefore they had every right to identify with the character because *in the fiction* the police were corrupt and therefore it was only 'natural human nature to approve of what the vigilante does'.

This approach is relatively sophisticated but nevertheless disingenuous. To say that it is only a story and that the narrative creates a space for identification is a perfectly sound position to take. But this identification must have impli-cations about the cadets' attitudes to crime, criminals and the law. The important point here is that the young want conservativism to be established through violence and force. This is not the attitude of a bureaucratic and routinised police force but of a small group who see danger on all sides, which must be violently eradicated. The attitude of these young policemen mirrors that of the older working- and middle-class groups, which suggests that these social and political attitudes structure identification.

5 A Taste for Horror

Taste, whether it be for clothes, house decoration or art, is a product of social experience. In the 1920s in an apparently esoteric study of the preferences for sweet as opposed to bitter chocolate amongst the Viennese working classes, Paul Lazarsfeld showed how their restricted purchasing power led them to select the immediate pleasures of sweet chocolate rather than the more subtle taste of 'bitter' chocolate.

Without being overly determinist, taste, even for food, is clearly linked to social location.

In our study we discovered that those who consider their work to be monotonous prefer horror films. The question therefore is, what is it about monotonous work, as opposed to non-monotonous work, that results in a taste for horror films? Why should it be that liking other kinds of films moves in the opposite direction?

By and large what people want from films has not changed over the years. Although the debate about 'video nasties' might make it appear as if most video-owners are sitting transfixed in front of *I Spit on Your Grave*, in terms of genre

TABLE 47

Type of film rented on the last three occasions

N = 975 (All rented video films)

| | Total | Montonous Work | |
		Agree	Disagree
Weighted Base	975	133	427
	%	%	%
Comedy	16	17	16
Science fiction	7	8	6
Horror	14	24	13
Cartoon	3	2	4
Adult film	3	6	2
Adventure	11	12	13
Thriller	13	14	13
Romance	5	1	5
Drama	7	3	9
Children's film	9	8	9
Musical	3	1	3
Other	6	3	7

TABLE 48

Hire of videograms by content category

N = 2,045

Percentage of market volume

	Purchases		Rentals	
Year	1983	1984	1983	1984
	%	%	%	%
Comedy	31	13	13	19
Comic/thriller	9	5	16	18
Musicals/music	5	20	2	18
Science fiction	4	11	4	8
General features	4	12	8	9
Adult	2	14	5	8
Horror	2	6	15	17
Sport	1	3	2	1
Children	–	1	5	7
Western/war	5	neg	21	13

(Rentals = last tape rented)
(*Source: NOP*)

most people want to see the same types of film as their parents and grandparents. But horror films do split the classes as a result of different social experiences and how those experiences are addressed by various types of films. The most important characteristic of horror films is a kind of controlled disruption. Although murder and mayhem are the horror film's stock-in-trade these elements are pushed out into a mythical reality. Notwithstanding the apparent 'reality' of these worlds they do not conform to the world in which the working class live. The natural and social orders are challenged and overturned in these films, but this does not affect the social order of the real 'lived' world. The horror film can function in a manner similar to a nursery rhyme or fairy tale: it tells stories about 'real' situations – parent/child conflict, long journeys to strange places, fear of animals – but by heightening reality can serve to reduce the fear. In other words, fears and anxieties are reduced by allowing them to be confronted through a process of disruption, but a disruption where the pain of resolution is rearranged so as not to create the sense that the audience's world is under threat.

It is not surprising that those with monotonous and boring jobs should value films that put surprise, change and transformation to the fore. What they might not be expected to appreciate are dreams of an anti-establishment type where the change offered is rooted in real challenges to the actuality of the existing social organisation. Their taste manifests an ambivalent position. Existing within a very tightly defined culture and within a social hierarchy, the boredom of their working life is irksome, and a film that breaks up that boredom, that disrupts social and psychological order, that makes a fool of authority without being too real, is enjoyed. The horror film operates as a fantasy challenge that is safely dangerous, a retreat from the horror of monotony, but containing its own message that the world is an ordered one, and that there is nothing out of place in the fact that their own lives are so rigorously ordered.

The attraction of horror films for those with monotonous jobs therefore is that they snap at authority without breaking it and, in disrupting the world without disturbing basic alignments, reflect the contradictions of their own lives. Hiring a video on Friday night signals that the routines of work are being left behind, but those with monotonous jobs cannot achieve – any more than anyone else – the dismantling of the psychological structures their work has created. Objectively the horror film is the 'escape' into the structure of order they wish to leave behind, even if subjectively it offers a temporary dislocation of order in the same way that Friday offers a temporary break from the ordered routine which is their unfortunate lot and to which they know they must return on Monday.

Video, however, at least gives a semblance of control over the structuring of their free time. It unshackles them from a dependence on the authority of broadcasting executives to decide what they shall watch on Friday night, the very moment they have broken with the authority of others to decide the pace of their lives. It is not by chance, however, and is an example of the subtlety of social control, that such individuals should exploit their freedom through the horror genre: their taste, regulated by the very rhythms of work from which they wish to escape, is for a form of film which is especially appropriate for the continuation of their condition.

6   I Prefer the Book

The pleasures people receive from films can be put in context by the pleasures taken in other forms of leisure. Given that film is supposed to be the consumate popular narrative art form of the 20th century, it is intriguing that the majority of discussants claimed they were 'invariably disappointed' by films based on books which they had read. Someone in the working-class group in London expressed disappointment over *Shogun*: 'First class book . . . [but] the film was naff' and a Harold Robbins novel, *59 Park Avenue*, where 'the character was changed from a big blonde-haired Polish bird to a dark-haired demure girl'. Similarly, a middle-class woman in York complained that William Styron's novel *Sophie's Choice* had been 'truncated and glamorised' in the film. Given the rhetoric about film being the most popular of art forms, it is interesting that the narrative structure and depth of characterisation in the traditional realist novel deliver pleasure more effectively than films. The Mills and Boon romances, bodice-rippers, Barbara Cartland, Harold

Robbins, Catherine Cookson, Barbara Taylor Bradford and others of that ilk may not be at the forefront of modern literature but they do provide pleasure, and, importantly, even with these types of books people are unhappy when they are translated into film.

Just as books seem to provide more narrative pleasure than films for our discussants, so pubs provided more social pleasure. According to one middle-class woman: 'the cinema is anti-social '. A student claimed that 'going to the pub is more of an occasion' and that it was better to 'make one's own fun'. Another middle-class discussant said: 'I prefer to be sitting talking to someone than watching a film.' A working-class Londoner said that if he was sitting watching a video and someone offered to take him for a pint he 'would be sorely tempted'. The consensus among our discussants was that they much preferred the company of other people to watching films. Pubs fit into the structure of leisure time more easily, and, because of that give more pleasure to more people than do films. It is quite clear from these last two examples that we cannot take for granted the pleasures which people receive from films.

Conclusion: Into the Future

Taste and pleasure are theoretical minefields, and although we do not pretend to have all the answers, we have been able to show the central importance of the family and the group experience in structuring taste and pleasure. An individual's life-cycle encourages social stability and rebellion, each of which leads to a certain relationship to film-watching as an activity, and to the content of films. In particular, film taste is located along two continua: conservative/radical and group/individual. The young are located roughly on the right-hand side of each continuum and, by and large, the cinema caters for them. The older groups have been catered for by television since the 1950s, but video and subscription movie services will rediscover conservative film taste, and the adult audience for film will re-emerge from behind the smokescreen of the young cinema audience. The future for feature films may yet throw up some surprises.

The future of work and the future of film audiences are intimately bound together. Skilled and semi-skilled working-class work is changing. On the bright side there are longer holidays, shorter working weeks, less overtime, increases in self-employed and part-time work. The dark side is that over half of those unemployed in the UK in the late 1980s have been so for over a year: long-term unemployment will have profound effects on leisure. Indeed, the future of leisure has become part of the great debate about post-industrial society. The collapse of Britain's manufacturing base, and the persistence of long-term unemployment for over three million people, has changed the character of working-class leisure. Furthermore, 96 per cent of the jobs lost in the UK have been in the north and as new jobs are predominantly in the service and professional sectors in the south-east, important regional variations in employment patterns will lead to similar variations in leisure.

Another regional factor which will have profound effects on film audiences is the decline of cinema provision outside of the south-east. Two-thirds of Scottish screens have disappeared since 1965, and half of those in the north of England, whereas the number in the outer metropolitan area of London has remained constant. In 1984 the south-east had 36 per cent of the country's screens, 48 per cent of the admissions (an increase of 12 per cent in its share since 1966), and, even more importantly, 53 per cent of the box office (an increase of 11 per cent).

Along with these social changes major technical developments will affect the future of film viewing. High-Definition Video and Video Disc, combined with flat screens, will provide similar quality to 35 mm prints in small cinemas and yet have the flexibility of a VCR. The quality of the viewing experience in the home will be better in some ways than that available today in many commercial cinemas.

The future for the cinema is difficult to predict. One thing alone is certain: whatever the technology which delivers feature films, the British public will continue to devour films with pleasure, discrimination and interest. The entertainment film remains an integral part of people's lives.

Appendix: Research Methodology

The central methodological task was to combine a quantifiable approach capable of providing a firm statistical basis by which to form generalisations about the audience, with qualitative techniques giving insight into people's attitudes to film. All statistical information in this study comes from our survey unless otherwise stated.

1 Qualitative Research

It was decided early in the research that not only did we wish for the richness of qualitative material, but that the information gained ought to inform the quantitative side of the study. The two techniques adopted in the more qualitative side were:

a) Group discussion

b) Q-sort attitude statements and factor analysis.

Before going into the field we piloted our group discussions. We wished the statements to be as naturalistic as possible. Thus, following the taping and transcribing of the pilot discussion a hundred and eight statements relating to film, leisure, occupational and family attitudes were drawn up. These were then checked and tested for internal consistency. Some alterations were made.

In all 10 discussion groups each consisting of between 8 and 14 people were organised. The groups were split by age

Q Sort Factors

Factor	Eigenvalue	Pct. of Var.	Cum. Pct.
1	13.73717	12.6	12.6
2	8.52797	7.8	20.4
3	6.94115	6.4	26.8
4	5.30744	4.9	31.7
5	4.88659	4.5	36.1
6	4.60884	4.2	40.4
7	3.74431	3.4	43.8
8	3.58176	3.3	47.1
9	3.33157	3.1	50.2

Cluster Profiles

	1 Cluster	2 Cluster	3 Cluster	4 Cluster
1. Factor 1	xxxxx.	xxxxxx.	.xx	.xxxxxx
2. Factor 2	xxxxxxx.	.xxx xx	.xxxxxxx	xxxxx.
3. Factor 3	x.	xxxxxxxxxxx.	.xx	.xxxxx
4. Factor 4	.xxx	xxxxxxxxxxx.	.xxx	xxxxxx.

Variable Loading

		Factor 1
4	0.6610	Films must be part of an evening out for me to enjoy them.
9	0.5305	If want to get out house for a while cinema is a convenient place to go.
7	0.5090	Films are the most enjoyable form of entertainment.

		Factor 2
5	0.7944	I like horror and adventure films which portray world as dangerous place.
3	0.7603	I can't enjoy films if they are very violent.

		Factor 3
16	0.7417	I daydream a lot about films and film characters.
14	0.7325	I sometimes try to behave like a character that I have seen in a film.
13	0.6141	Films can make you feel discontented with life.

(under 16; 17 and over), class, (ABC1 and C2DE) and region (North and South). Most discussions lasted about two hours, followed by the administration of two questionnaires: one relating to the respondent's occupation and demographic circumstances, the other consisting of the 108 attitude statement drawn from the pilot discussion groups. The answers to these were then factor-analysed. The main discriminatory attitude statements were then used to form part of our main national survey, the results of which we subsequently cluster analysed to explore the distribution of public taste.

2   Quantitative Research

Originally it was our intention to conduct only one national survey but it became apparent early in the research that the existing lack of information about the audience was insufficient to allow the construction of quota samples. Some preliminary data was necessary. Thus, in December 1984 we commissioned NOP to ask, via their weekly omnibus survey, (sample size 2,000) a series of questions to determine the universe to be sampled.

The main national survey took place in December 1984. Although originally envisaged that the sample size would be of about a thousand people, it was decided to reduce the number to eight hundred. This was made possible through the knowledge gained from the omnibus questions. Without losing predictability and the ability to generalise to the population as a whole the advantage in reducing the sample was that of increasing the length of the questionnaire and thus gaining more information.

Following the main survey a further two surveys were conducted: one to the general audience; the other to a specialist audience.

Given the rapid uptake in video recorders it was decided towards the end of the study in 1986 to again take advantage of NOP's weekly omnibus survey and place questions to determine changes in patterns of viewing as well as check questions in the main survey.

The 'specialist' survey involved 2,200 people who attended 13 Regional Film Theatres. The idea to include such individuals in the frame of analysis emerged from findings in the body of the main survey relating to the influence of education and occupation on film taste and cinema attendance; did those committed to the cinema offer insight into general cinema attendance?

The survey was administered by the Broadcasting Research Unit. The computer analysis was done by Dr Steven Tagg at the Social Statistics Laboratory, University of Stathclyde.

The questionnaire is reproduced opposite.

SERIAL NO: _____

CINEMA   (6-9)

NAME: _____   1 (10)

ADDRESS: _____

_____

_____ TEL. NO: _____

OCCUPATION OF HEAD OF HOUSEHOLD: _____

	AB	C1	C2	DE	
	1	2	3	4	(11)

Q.1 Have you been to the cinema in the last twelve months, that is since November 1983?

(12)
Yes ------------------------ 1 (12)
No ------------------------- 2

Q.2 Does your household have a video cassette recorder?

(13)
Yes ------------------------ 1 (13)
No ------------------------- 2

CHECK QUOTAS, AND ONLY CONTINUE IF RESPONDENT FITS QUOTA.

ASK ALL

Q.3 SHOWCARD A Have you seen any of these films at the cinema? Do not include films seen on video or television. Any others?

(14)
The Return of the Jedi --- 1
Superman III ------------- 2 (14)
Never Say Never Again ---- 3
Octopussy ---------------- 4 ASK Q.4
ET ----------------------- 5
Ghandi ------------------- 6
Indiana Jones and the
  Temple of Doom --------- 7
Grey Stoke --------------- 8
Terms of Endearment ------ 9
Company of Wolves -------- 0
1984 --------------------- X
None of these ------------ Y GO TO
                            FILTER
                            BEFORE
                            Q.6

Q.4 Who did you go with on the last time you saw one of the films on the card? Anyone else?

Q.5 Who chose the film on this occasion? IF JOINT DECISION CODE ALL THAT APPLY.

	Q.4	Q.5	
	(15)	(16)	
Mother --------------	1	1	
Father --------------	2	2	(15/
Brother -------------	3	3	16)
Sister --------------	4	4	
Husband/wife --------	5	ASK 5	
Boyfriend/girlfriend -	6	Q.5 6	
Friends (same sex) ---	7	7	
Friends (opposite sex)	8	8	
Children ------------	9	9	
Other ---------------	0	0	
No one --------------	X	GO	
		TO FILTER	
		BEFORE	
Respondent ----------		Q.6 Y	

IF RESPONDENT HAS BEEN TO CINEMA IN PAST YEAR (CHECK Q.1) ASK Q.6, IF NOT GO TO Q.24.

Q.6 SHOWCARD B How often do you go to the cinema nowadays?

(17)
Once a week or more -------- 1
Two to three times a month - 2 (17)
Once a month --------------- 3
Once every two months ------ 4
Four or five times a year -- 5
Two or three times a year -- 6
Once a year ---------------- 7

Q.7 How many times have you been to the cinema in the last four months, that is since August?

(18)
Once ----------------------- 1 (18)
Twice ---------------------- 2
Three times ---------------- 3
Four times ----------------- 4
Five or more times --------- 5
None ----------------------- 6

125

SHOWCARD A AGAIN

Q8a   Apart from any of the films on the card, what film did you see the last time you went to the cinema?

Q8b   Who did you go with on that occasion? Anyone else?

Q8c   SHOWCARD A AGAIN Again apart from any of the films on the card, what film did you see the time before that?

Q8d   And who did you go with on that occasion? Anyone else?

Q8e   What film did you see the time before that?

Q8f   And who did you go with on that occasion? Anyone else?

	Q8a/b	Q8c/d	Q8e/f
Film	_____	_____	_____
	_____	_____	_____

Who with	(19)	(20)	(21)	
Mother	1	1	1	
Father	2	2	2	[19/21]
Brother	3	3	3	
Sister	4	4	4	
Children	5	5	5	
Husband/wife	6	6	6	
Boy/girlfriend	7	7	7	
Friends (same sex)	8	8	8	
Friends (opposite sex)	9	9	9	
Other	0	0	0	
No one	X	X	X	

Q9a Is there a particular day that you like to go to the cinema on? Which day? CAN BE MULTI CODED.

(22)

Yes - Monday ------------ 1   (22)
       Tuesday ------------ 2
       Wednesday --------- 3
       Thursday ---------- 4 ASK Q9b
       Friday ------------ 5
       Saturday ---------- 6
       Sunday ------------ 7
No -------------------- 8 GO TO Q.10

Q10 Do you ever go to .... READ OUT.

	Yes	No	
Regional Film Theatres	1	2	(24)
Specialist cinemas, showing foreign films or less well-known films	1	2	(25)

Q9b Why do you prefer that day? PROBE FULLY. Why is that? Any other reasons?

_____ (23)
     1 2 3 4
_____ 5 6 7 8
     9 0 X Y
_____

_____

OFFICE USE ONLY

(26)	(27)	(28)
1 2 3 4	1 2 3 4	1 2 3 4
5 6 7 8	5 6 7 8	5 6 7 8
9 0 X Y	9 0 X Y	9 0 X Y

(29)	(30)	(31)
1 2 3 4	1 2 3 4	1 2 3 4
5 6 7 8	5 6 7 8	5 6 7 8
9 0 X Y	9 0 X Y	9 0 X Y

Q11 SHOWCARD C When you go to the cinema do you normally do any of these things as well?

	(32)
Have a meal out before or afterwards	1 (32)
Go to a pub for a drink before or afterwards	2
Get a take-away meal afterwards	3
None of these things	4

Q12 Is there a local cinema you can go to?

	(33)
Yes	1 (33)
No	2

Q13 Approximately how far away is your nearest cinema?

	(34)
Less than 1 mile	1 (34)
One mile and less than 2 miles	2
2 miles and less than 4 miles	3
4 miles or more	4
No idea	5

Q14 Is this the one you visit most often?

	(35)
Yes	1 (35)
No	2

Q15 Would you go to the cinema more often if there was a cinema nearer to you?

	(36)
Yes	1 (36)
No	2
Don't know	3

Q16 How do you usually get to the cinema?

	(37)
Walk	1 (37)
Car	2
Bicycle/motorcycle	3
Public transport	4
Taxi	5

Q17 How much was your ticket the last time you went to the cinema?

```
        (38)     (39)(40)       (38/
   £  [      ]  [      ][      ]   40)

   Don't know = X.XX
```

Q18 SHOWCARD D Which of these did you do the last time you went out in the evening?

	(41)	
Went to a pub or wine bar	1	(41)
Went to a night club or disco	2	ASK
Went to the theatre	3	Q19a
Went to a concert	4	
Had a meal out	5	
None of these	6	GO TO Q20

Q19a How much did you personally spend on that occasion? IF 'NOTHING' CODE 00.00 AND ASK Q19b. OTHERS CODE AMOUNT AND GO TO Q20.

```
        (42)(43)     (44)(45)       (42/
   £  [      ][      ]  [      ][      ]   45)

   Don't know = XX.XX
```

IF RESPONDENT SPENT NOTHING ASK Q19b. OTHERS GO TO Q20

Q19b Approximately how much was spent on your behalf?

```
        (46)(47)     (48)(49)       (46/
   £  [      ][      ]  [      ][      ]   49)

   Don't know = XX.XX
```

Q20 Do you think the cinema is good or bad value for money compared to other forms of entertainment?

	(50)
Good value	1
Bad value	2
About the same	3 (50)
Don't know	4

Q21 Do you read reviews of films in ... READ OUT EACH IN TURN.

	Yes	No	
a) newspapers	1	5	
b) magazines	2	6	(51)
c) specialist film magazines	3	7	
d) music papers	4	8	

Q22 Do you ever watch.... READ OUT

	Yes	No	
a) Film 84 on BBC1	1	4	
b) Visions on Channel 4	2	5	(52)
c) Electric Theatre on ITV	3	6	

127

Q23a <u>SHOWCARD E</u> Which of these influences you most in deciding which film
to see? <u>CODE ONE ONLY BELOW.</u>

Q23b <u>SHOWCARD E</u> Which others are also important?

	Q.23a	Q.23b
	(53)	(54)
What friends say about it ----------	1 -------	1
Reading/seeing reviews -------------	2 -------	2
Seeing adverts in newspapers -------	3 -------	3
Seeing adverts on television -------	4 -------	4
Seeing previews at the cinema ------	5 -------	5
Seeing posters ---------------------	6 -------	6
Reading newspapers articles --------	7 -------	7
Whatever is on the night I want to go out -----------------------------	8 -------	8
Other (WRITE IN)		
_____	9	9
None -------------------------------	0 -------	0
Don't know -------------------------	X -------	X

(53/54)

<u>ASK ALL</u>

Q24 Are there any reasons why you don't go to the cinema more often?
What are they?

_____

_____

_____

(55)
1 2 3 4
5 6 7 8
9 0 X Y

IF RESPONDENT HAS A VIDEO RECORDER ASK Q25.   OTHERS GO TO Q.46

Q25 Is your video recorder owned or rented?   (56)

Owned ----------------- 1
Rented ---------------- 2

(56)

Q26a <u>SHOWCARD F</u> Which of these was the most important reason why your household
got a video recorder? CODE ONE ONLY BELOW.

Q26b <u>SHOWCARD F</u> Which other reasons were important in deciding to get a video
recorder?

	Q.26a	Q.26b
	(57)	(58)
To tape sports programmes ----------	1 -------	1
To tape films ----------------------	2 -------	2
To tape other programmes -----------	3 -------	3
To rent feature films --------------	4 -------	4
To watch adult videos --------------	5 -------	5
My friends all have one ------------	6 -------	6
The children wanted one ------------	7 -------	7
To fit in with difficult working hours ------------------------------	8 -------	8
Too much rubbish on TV -------------	9 -------	9
To use video camera ----------------	0 -------	0
Other (WRITE IN)		
_____ ___ _____	X	X
Don't know -------------------------	Y -------	Y

(57/58)

128

Q27a How long have you had a video recorder?   (59)

                                    Less than 3 months ------------------ 1
                                    3 months and less than 6 months ----- 2   (59)
                                    6 months and less than 1 year ------- 3
                                    1 year and less than 2 years -------- 4
                                    2 years or more -------------------- 5

Q27b <u>SHOWCARD G</u> What do you mainly   Recording sports programmes --------- 1
     use your video for?   Recording films ---------------------- 2
                                          Recording educational programmes ---- 3   (60)
                                          Recording other programmes ---------- 4
                                          Renting feature films --------------- 5
                                          Using video camera ------------------ 6
                                          Other (WRITE IN)

                                          _____ 7

                                          Don't know ------------------------- 8

Q28a Do you ever record films from   Q28a   Q28b
     the television that you keep,   (61)   (62)
     rather than just watching and   No - never -------------- 1 ------- 1
     then recoding   How often   Yes - more than once a week 2 ------- 2   (61/62)
     do you do this?   once a week --------- 3 ------- 3
                                            once a fortnight ---- 4 ------- 4
Q28b Do you ever record films from   once a month -------- 5 ------- 5
     television   that you never   less often ---------- 6 ------- 6
     get round to watching, and
     record over them without
     watching? How often?

Q29 Do you or your family ever hire   (63)
     or rent video films? How often?   No - never --------------- 1 GO TO Q41
                                        Yes - 4 or more times a   (63)
                                              week --------------- 2
                                            - 1-3 times a week ---- 3 ASK Q30
                                            - 1-3 times a month --- 4
                                            - Once every 2 or 3
                                              months ------------- 5
                                            - Less often --------- 6

Q30 Do you rent more films than you   (64)
     did when you first got your   More -------------------------------- 1
     video recorder, or fewer, or   Fewer ------------------------------- 2   (64)
     about the same?   Same -------------------------------- 3
                                      Don't know -------------------------- 4

Q31 <u>SHOWCARD H</u> What type of film was the last one you rented? And the one before
     that? And the one before that?

                                    Last one   Last but one Last but two
     Comedy ----------------------------(65)------- (66)---------- (67)-------- 1
     Science Fiction ----------------------- 2 --------- 2 ----------- 2   (65/67)
     Horror -------------------------------- 3 --------- 3 ----------- 3
     Cartoon ------------------------------- 4 --------- 4 ----------- 4
     Adult Film ---------------------------- 5 --------- 5 ----------- 5
     Adventure ----------------------------- 6 --------- 6 ----------- 6
     Thriller ------------------------------ 7 --------- 7 ----------- 7
     Romance ------------------------------- 8 --------- 8 ----------- 8
     Drama --------------------------------- 9 --------- 9 ----------- 9
     Children's film ----------------------- 0 --------- 0 ----------- 0
     Musical ------------------------------- X --------- X ----------- X
     Other (WRITE IN)

     _____ Y _____ Y _____ Y

129

Q32 The last time you rented a video film did you watch it with anyone else?

    a)   with how many people, including yourself?

    b)   who did you watch it with?

Q32c Who chose the last film that you rented? IF JOINT DECISION CODE ALL THAT
     APPLY.

	Q32a (68)		Q32b (69)	Q32c (70)	
One (self only)	1	Mother	1	1	(68)
Two	2	Father	2	2	/
Three	3	Brother	3	3	70)
Four	4	Sister	4	4	
Five	5	Husband/wife	5	5	
Six	6	Boyfriend/girlfriend	6	6	
Seven	7	Friends (same sex)	7	7	
Eight or more	8	Friends (opposite sex)	8	8	
RING AND WRITE IN		Children	9	9	
		Other	0	0	
_____	9	No one	X	X	
Don't know	0	Respondent		Y	

Q33a Is there a particular day that you   Yes - Monday ---------- 1
     like to watch video films on?   Tuesday --------- 2
     Which day? CAN BE MULTI-CODED.   Wednesday ------- 3 ASK   (71)
                                                     Thursday -------- 4 Q33b
                                                     Friday ---------- 5
                                                     Saturday -------- 6
                                                     Sunday ---------- 7
                                              No ------------------ 8 GO TO Q34

Q33b Why do you prefer that day? PROBE FULLY Why is that? Any other reasons?

_____   (72)
                                                        1 2 3 4
_____   5 6 7 8
                                                        9 0 X Y
_____

_____

                                                        (73)
Q34   Is there a particular time of day   Yes - morning ---------------------- 1   (73)
      when you like to watch video films?   afternoon ------------------- 2
      CAN BE MULTI-CODED   evening --------------------- 3
                                                   late at night --------------- 4
                                             No ---------------------------------- 5

                                                        (74)
Q35   Do you usually watch video films
      in your own home or at a friends   Own house ------------------------ 1   (74)
      or relatives?   Friend's/relatives --------------- 2
                                             Both equally --------------------- 3

                                                        (75)
Q36   Where do you rent your video
      films from?   Local video shop ----------------- 1   (75)
                                             Video shop in town/city centre --- 2
                                             Newsagent ------------------------ 3
                                             Other (WRITE IN)

                                             _____ 4

130

Q37 SHOWCARD I Which of these do you
usually do when you rent a video
film?

(76)
Make sure the children are in bed ---- 1 (76)
Get a take-away meal ----------------- 2
Take the 'phone off the hook --------- 3
Invite friends round ----------------- 4
Turn off the lights ------------------ 5
Have a drink ------------------------- 6
None of these ------------------------ 7

Q38 How much do you normally pay to
rent a video film?

(77) (78) (79)   (77/
£ ☐☐ . ☐☐ p   79)
Don't know = X.XX   (80)

Q39 Do you think that rental video
films are good or bad value for
money compared with other forms
of entertainment?

Good -------------------------------- 1 (80)
Bad --------------------------------- 2
About the same ---------------------- 3
                    NEW CARD. DUP COLS.
                    1-9 ② (10)

Q40 SHOWCARD J How would you rate
the quality of films available
for hire on video? (I do not
mean the technical quality of
the video tape, but whether
the films themselves are good).

Very good --------------------------- 1 (11)
Fairly good ------------------------- 2 (11)
Fairly poor ------------------------- 3
Very poor --------------------------- 4
Don't know -------------------------- 5

ASK ALL VIDEO-OWNERS

Q41 Have you ever bought pre-recorded
feature films on video? How many?

(12)
No - none ------------------ 1 GO TO Q43 (12)
Yes - one ------------------- 2
      two ------------------- 3 ASK
      three-five ------------ 4 Q42
      six-ten --------------- 5
      eleven or more -------- 6

Q42 Why did you decide to buy those films rather than renting them?
Any other reason?

_____
_____   (13)
_____   1 2 3 4
_____   5 6 7 8
                                                      9 0 X Y
_____
_____

Q43 Would you say you go to the cinema
more than you did before you had a
video, or less than before, or has
the video made no difference?

(14)
More -------------------------------- 1
Less -------------------------------- 2 (14)
No difference ----------------------- 3
Don't know -------------------------- 4

Q44a Do your family spend more or less
leisure time together since getting
a video, or has it made no difference?
PROMPT AS NECESSARY

(15)
Much more --------------------------- 1 (15)
Slightly more ----------------------- 2
No difference ----------------------- 3
Slightly less ----------------------- 4
Much less --------------------------- 5
Don't know -------------------------- 6
Does not apply ---------------------- 7

Q44b Overall how satisfied or dissatisfied are you with your
video recorder? READ OUT:

(16)
Very satisfied ---------------------- 1 (16)
Fairly satisfied -------------------- 2
Fairly dissatisfied ----------------- 3
or Very dissatisfied ----------------- 4
(Don't know) ------------------------ 5

131

Q45 Not counting any films that you rent or buy, do you watch more or less television since getting a video, or has it made no difference? PROMPT AS NECESSARY.

(17)

Much more	1	(17)
Slightly more	2	NOW
No difference	3	GO
Slightly less	4	TO
Much less	5	Q49
Don't know	6	

ASK ALL NON VIDEO-OWNERS

Q46 Would you like to have a video recorder, or not?

(18)

Yes	1	ASK Q47a	(18)
No	2	GO TO
Don't know	3	Q48

Q47a Is there any particular reason why you have not got a video recorder?

(19)

Too expensive ----------------------- 1 (19)
Not got round to it ---------------- 2
Other (WRITE IN)

_____

_____ 3

Q47b SHOWCARD K Why would you like to have a video recorder?

(20)

To tape sports programmes --------- 1 (20)
To tape films ---------------------- 2
To tape other programmes ----------- 3
To rent feature films -------------- 4
To watch adult videos ------------- 5
My friends all have one ----------- 6
The children wanted one ----------- 7
To fit in with difficult working
  hours ---------------------------- 8
Too much rubbish on TV ------------ 9
Other (WRITE IN)

_____ 0

Don't know ------------------------- X

Q48 Do you ever get together with friends who have a video recorder to watch films? How often?

(21)

Once a week or more ---------------- 1 (21)
Two to three times a month -------- 2
Once a month ----------------------- 3
Four or five times a year --------- 4
Two or three times a year --------- 5
Once a year or less --------------- 6
Never ------------------------------ 7

ASK ALL

Q49 Do you look at the TV Times, Radio Times, the television page of the newspaper or Ceefax or Oracle to make certain that you know what films are on television? PROMPT AS NECESSARY.

(22)

Yes - every day --------------------- 1 (22)
    - most days --------------------- 2
    - some days --------------------- 3
No - never ------------------------- 4

Q50 If there is a film on television that you want to see, do you always make a special effort to see it, or do you usually make a special effort, or sometimes, or never?

(23)

Yes - always ----------------------- 1 (23)
    - usually ---------------------- 2
    - sometimes ------------------- 3
No - never ------------------------ 4

Q51 SHOWCARD L Did you see (or video) any of these films on television in the last couple of weeks? Any others? IF RESPONDENT HAS VIDEO RECORDER PROMPT FOR EACH FILM TO FIND OUT IF WATCHED LIVE, VIDEOED AND WATCHED, OR VIDEOED AND NOT WATCHED.

Films	WATCHED LIVE	VIDEOED AND WATCHED	VIDEOED AND NOT WATCHED
	(24)	(27)	(30)
1 Tunisan Victory	1	1	1 (24/
2 The Silent Village	2	2	2 32)
3 Daughters Courageous	3	3	3
4 The Draughtsman's Contract	4	4	4
5 Assignment Redhead	5	5	5
6 The Grasshopper	6	6	6
7 Victory	7	7	7
8 One More River	8	8	8
9 Sphinx	9	9	9
10 Nightmare	0	0	0
11 Battle of the Bulge	X	X	X
12 Jassy	Y	Y	Y
	(25)	(28)	(31)
13 Rooney	1	1	1
14 Noah's Ark	2	2	2
15 The 2 Worlds of Jennie Logan	3	3	3
16 Helter Skelter	4	4	4
17 Three for All	5	5	5
18 The Bachelor Party	6	6	6
19 Ziegfield Girl	7	7	7
20 Three Little Worlds	8	8	8
21 Picone Sent Me	9	9	9
22 Logan's Run	0	0	0
23 Lady from Shanghai	X	X	X
24 Carbon Copy	Y	Y	Y
	(26)	(29)	(32)
25 Playmates	1	1	1
26 The Devil's Advocate	2	2	2
27 The Return of Peter Grimm	3	3	3
28 George White's Scandals	4	4	4
29 Paradise Alley	5	5	5
None	X	X	X
Can't remember	Y	Y	Y

132

Q52a The last time you watched a feature film on the television, who did you watch with? Anyone else?

Q52b And who chose the film that you watched on that occasion? IF JOINT DECISION CODE ALL THAT APPLY.

	Q52a (33)	Q52b (34)	
Mother	1	1	
Father	2	2	(33/
Brother	3	3	34)
Sister	4	4	
Husband/wife	5	5	
Boyfriend/girlfriend	6	6	
Friends (same sex)	7	7	
Friends (opposite sex)	8	8	
Children	9	9	
Other	0	0	
No one	X	-	
Respondent	-	Y	

Q53 Do you think there are too many films on television, or not enough, or is the number of films on television about right?

```
                                   (35)
Too many ------------------------ 1   (35)
Too few ------------------------- 2
About right --------------------- 3
Don't know ---------------------- 4
```

Q54 SHOWCARD M If there is a particular film on television that you want to see, do you do any of these things while you're watching?

```
                                   (36)
Have a drink -------------------- 1   (36)
Get a take-away meal ------------ 2
Invite friends round ------------ 3
Make sure the children are in
  bed --------------------------- 4
Turn off the lights ------------- 5
Take the phone off the hook ----- 6
None of these ------------------- 7
```

Q55 Which of these do you think is the best way to watch a feature film? READ OUT.

```
                                   (37)
In the cinema ---------- 1 ASK Q56   (37)
On a video recorder at
  home ----------------- 2 GO TO Q57
or on television at home -- 3 GO TO Q58
(Don't know) ----------- 4 GO TO Q59a
```

IF BEST IN CINEMA

Q56 Why is that?

```
                            (38)
Atmosphere ------------ 1       (38)
Darkness -------------- 2
Large screen ---------- 3 NOW
Presence of crowd ----- 4 GO
Better sound ---------- 5 TO
Better picture -------- 6 Q59a
More comfortable ------ 7
Like to go out -------- 8
Other (WRITE IN)

_____ 9

Don't know ------------ 0
```

IF BETTER ON VIDEO

Q57 Why is that?

```
                            (39)
Freedom to watch when
  you want ------------- 1      (39)
Choice of films ------- 2 NOW
Chance to stop/rewind
  etc. ---------------- 3 GO
Don't need to go out -- 4 TO
Cheaper --------------- 5 Q59a
Other (WRITE IN)

_____ 6

Don't know ------------ 7
```

IF BETTER ON TELEVISION

Q58 Why is that?

```
                                 (40)
Convenient/no work ------------ 1
Don't need to go out ---------- 2 (40)
Better quality (than video) --- 3
Cheaper ----------------------- 4
Other (WRITE IN)

_____ 5

Don't know -------------------- 6
```

133

Q59a <u>SHOWCARD N</u> Which of these are most important to you in deciding whether to see a film or not? CODE ONE ONLY BELOW.

Q59b <u>SHOWCARD N</u> And which others are important?

	Q59a (41)	Q59b (42)	
Plot/storyline	1	1	(41/42)
Type of film/genre	2	2	
Acting/stars	3	3	
Photography	4	4	
Music	5	5	
Scenery/setting	6	6	
Special effects	7	7	
Writer	8	8	
Director	9	9	
Producer	0	0	
None of these	X	X	
Don't know	Y	Y	

Q60a Who is your favourite TV star?

(43)
1 2 3 4
5 6 7 8
9 0 X Y

Q60 Who is your favourite film star?

(44)
1 2 3 4
5 6 7 8
9 0 X Y

Q61 Why is he/she your favourite film star?

(45)
1 2 3 4
5 6 7 8
9 0 X Y

(46)
1 2 3 4
5 6 7 8
9 0 X Y

(47)
1 2 3 4
5 6 7 8
9 0 X Y

Q62 <u>SHOWCARD O</u> Which of these characteristics best describes what you like about him/her? Please read out the number of any that apply.

(48)(49)	(50) (51)	(52)(53)	(54)(55)	(56)(57)	(58)(59)	(48/59)

Q63 <u>SHOWCARD P</u> What are your three favourite types of film?

	1st Mentioned (60)	2nd Mentioned (61)	3rd Mentioned (62)	
Comedy	1	1	1	(60/62)
Science Fiction	2	2	2	
Horror	3	3	3	
War	4	4	4	
Adult Films	5	5	5	
Western	6	6	6	
Thriller	7	7	7	
Romance	8	8	8	
Drama	9	9	9	
Adventure	0	0	0	
Musical	X	X	X	
Other (WRITE IN)				
	Y	Y	Y	

Q64 <u>SHOWCARD Q</u> I am going to read out a number of statements people have made
<u>about films</u>, and for each one I would like you to tell me how strongly you
agree or disagree with it?

		Agree strongly	<u>Agree</u>	Neither agree nor disagree	Disagree	Disagree strongly	Don't know	
a)	I don't like films with a complicated plot	1	2	3	4	5	6	(63)
b)	I prefer films that have a message	1	2	3	4	5	6	(64)
c)	I can't enjoy films if they are very violent	1	2	3	4	5	6	(65)
d)	Films must be part of an evening out for me to enjoy them	1	2	3	4	5	6	(66)
e)	I like horror and adventure films which portray the world as a dangerous place	1	2	3	4	5	6	(67)
f)	My own problems are put into perspective when I watch a film	1	2	3	4	5	6	(68)
g)	Films are the most enjoyable form of entertainment	1	2	3	4	5	6	(69)
h)	If a film is good I don't mind where I watch it	1	2	3	4	5	6	(70)
i)	If I want to get out of the house for a while the cinema is a convenient place to go	1	2	3	4	5	6	(71)
j)	I don't mind if a film is slow-moving so long as it interests me	1	2	3	4	5	6	(72)
k)	Going to the cinema is only enjoyable if you are with someone else	1	2	3	4	5	6	(73)
l)	I only go to the cinema when I'm at a loose end	1	2	3	4	5	6	(74)
m)	Films can make you feel discontented with life	1	2	3	4	5	6	(75)
n)	I sometimes try to behave like a character that I have seen in a film	1	2	3	4	5	6	(76)
o)	I like films which criticise authority	1	2	3	4	5	6	(77)
p)	I daydream a lot about films and film characters	1	2	3	4	5	6	(78)
q)	I prefer films with British characters and British settings	1	2	3	4	5	6	(79)

Q65 SHOWCARD R Which three of these types of television programmes do you like best?

	1st Mentioned	2nd Mentioned	3rd Mentioned	
	(12)	(14)	(16)	③ (10)
Soap operas	1	1	1	SKIP COL 11
Situation comedies	2	2	2	
Other comedy programmes	3	3	3	
Variety shows	4	4	4	(12/17)
Quiz shows	5	5	5	
Sports	6	6	6	
News	7	7	7	
Wildlife programmes	8	8	8	
Documentaries	9	9	9	
Feature films	0	0	0	
Game shows	X	X	X	
Chat shows	Y	Y	Y	
	(13)	(15)	(17)	
Travel programmes	1	1	1	
Religious programmes	2	2	2	
Other (WRITE IN)				
	3	3	3	
Don't know	4	4	4	

Q66 SHOWCARD S How would you rate the quality of films shown in the cinema nowadays? (I do not mean the technical quality of the film, but whether the film itself is good or bad).

(18)
Very good	1	(18)
Fairly good	2	
Fairly poor	3	
Very poor	4	
Don't know	5	

Q67 Do you ever read books for pleasure nowadays - I mean other than for work or school?

(19)
| Yes | 1 ASK Q68 | (19) |
| No | 2 GO TO Q70 | |

Q68 How many books would you say you read from cover to cover in an average month?

(20)
One or less	1	(20)
Two or three	2	
Four or five	3	
Six to ten	4	
Over ten	5	
Don't know	6	

Q70 What type of book do you read most often?

(21)
Non-fiction	1	(21)
Thriller/crime	2	
Romance	3	
Adventure	4	
Historical novels	5	
General novels	6	
Other (WRITE IN)		
	7	
Don't know	8	

(22)

Q70 How many hours a day do you   Don't listen -------------- 1 GO TO Q72a
     listen to the radio, on average?   Under 1 -------------------- 2
                                          1 - 2 --------------------- 3   ASK   (22)
                                          3 - 4 --------------------- 4   Q71
                                          5 hours or more ----------- 5
                                          Don't know --------------- 6
                                                                                    (23)
Q71 Which radio station do you listen   Radio 1 ------------------------------- 1
     to most?   Radio 2 ------------------------------- 2 (23)
                                          Radio 3 ------------------------------- 3
                                          Radio 4 ------------------------------- 4
                                          BBC Local radio ----------------------- 5
                                          ILR (commercial) ---------------------- 6
                                          Other --------------------------------- 7

Q72a SHOWCARD T Could you look at the various activities on this card and tell me
     all the ones you ever do nowadays? Any others?

     FOR EACH ONE DONE ASK Q72b AND 72c

Q72b SHOWCARD U How often nowadays do you .... (ACTIVITY) RECORD BELOW

Q72c Can you tell me who you usually ..... (ACTIVITY) with? Anyone else?

	Q72a		Q72b						Q72c			
	Ever do	Every day	Several days a week	Once a week	Once a fort-night	Once a month	Less often	Alone	With spouse	With family	With friends	With others
Play sport/ keep fit ---	1	2 ---	3 ----	4 ---	5 ----	6 ---	7 --	8 ----	9 -----	0 ----	X ---	Y (24)
Watch sport (not on TV).	1	2 ---	3 ----	4 ---	5 ----	6 ---	7 --	8 ----	9 -----	0 ----	X ---	Y (25)
Go to theatre/ concerts ---	1	2 ---	3 ----	4 ---	5 ----	6 ---	7 --	8 ----	9 -----	0 ----	X ---	Y (26)
Go out for a meal -------	1	2 ---	3 ----	4 ---	5 ----	6 ---	7 --	8 ----	9 -----	0 ----	X ---	Y (27)
Go to pub/ wine bar ---	1	2 ---	3 ----	4 ---	5 ---	6 ----	7 --	8 ----	9 -----	0 ----	X ---	Y (28)
Go to disco/ night club -	1	2 ---	3 ----	4 ---	5 ---	6 ----	7 --	8 ----	9 -----	0 ----	X ---	Y (29)
Go to evening classes/clubs societies/ voluntary work -------	1	2 ---	3 ----	4 ---	5 ---	6 ----	7 --	8 ----	9 -----	0 ----	X ---	Y (30)
Visit friends/ relatives --	1	2 ---	3 ----	4 ---	5 ---	6 ----	7 --	8 ----	9 -----	0 ----	X ---	Y (31)
Go to parties.	1	2 ---	3 ----	4 ---	5 ---	6 ----	7 --	8 ----	9 -----	0 ----	X ---	Y (32)
None of these	N GO TO Q73a											

Q73a SHOWCARD V And which of these activities do you do nowadays? Any others?

FOR EACH ONE DONE ASK Q73b

Q73b SHOWCARD W How often nowadays do you .... (ACTIVITY)

	Ever do	Every day	Several days a week	Once a week	Once a fortnight	Once a month	Less often	
Read magazines/news-papers	1	2	3	4	5	6	7	(33)
Watch television	1	2	3	4	5	6	7	(34)
Listen to records	1	2	3	4	5	6	7	(35)
Have visits from friends/relatives	1	2	3	4	5	6	7	(36)
Sew/knit/garden/DIY	1	2	3	4	5	6	7	(37)
Spend time on hobbies	1	2	3	4	5	6	7	(38)

None of these ------------ N GO TO Q74

Q74 SHOWCARD X People have different ideas about the facilities which a local community needs. Can you tell me which of these you think are essential for a local community?

IF MORE THAN THREE MENTIONED ASK Q75

Q75 And which two or three do you think are most important?

	Q74 All (39)	Q75 Top 2 or 3 (41)	
Pub/wine bar	1	1	(39/
Fish and chip shop/take away	2	2	42)
Disco	3	3	
Bingo hall	4	4	
Cinema	5	5	
Cafe/Restaurant	6	6	
Swimming pool	7	7	
Social club	8	8	
Library	9	9	
Leisure/sports centre	0	0	
Video hire shop	X	X	
Youth Club	Y	Y	
	(40)	(42)	
Park/open space	1	1	

Other (WRITE IN)

_____ 2 ------------ 2
Don't know -------------------------- 3 ---------- 3

(43)

Q76 Thinking of the people who live in this area how many would you regard as friends or acquaintances? READ OUT.

Most of them ------------- 1
Some of them ------------- 2 ASK Q77 (43)
Just a few of them -------- 3
or None of them ------------ 4 GO TO Q78

(44)

Q77 How often do you see them socially - I mean go round to their house for a coffee or for a meal, or have them round to your house, or go out somewhere together?

More than once a week ------------- 1
Once a week ------------------------ 2 (44)
Once a fortnight ------------------- 3
Once a month ----------------------- 4
Less often ------------------------- 5
Never ------------------------------ 6

ASK ALL

Q78 I am going to read out some facilities which are sometimes subsidised by central or local government. For each one can you tell me if you think they ought to be subsidised or not?

	Yes	No	Don't know
Theatres	1	2	3
Libraries	4	5	6
Swimming pools	7	8	9	(45)
Sports centres	1	2	3
Art galleries	4	5	6
Cinemas	7	8	9	(46)

(47)

Q79 I would finally like to ask you a few questions to help us analyse the results. Are you ...... READ OUT.

Single ------------------- 1 ASK Q80 (47)
Married ------------------ 2 GO TO Q82
Separated ---------------- 3
Divorced ----------------- 4 GO TO Q83
or Widowed ----------------- 5

(48)

Q80 Do you live alone or do you live with your parents or do you share with friends?

Alone ------------------- 1
Parents ----------------- 2   BOTH IN COL. 48
Friends ----------------- 3

Q81 Do you have a regular boyfriend/girlfriend?

Yes ----------------------- X ASK Q82
No ------------------------ Y GO TO Q84

ASK IF MARRIED OR WITH REGULAR BOYFRIEND/GIRLFRIEND. OTHERS GO TO FILTER BEFORE Q83.

(49)

Q82 How long have you been married/with your present partner?

Under a year ----------------------- 1 (49)
1 - 2 years ------------------------- 2
3 - 5 years ------------------------- 3
Over 5 years ------------------------ 4

IF MARRIED, SEPARATED, WIDOWED OR DIVORCED ASK Q83. OTHERS GO TO Q84

(50)

Q83 Do you have any children living at home with you? PROBE AS NECESSARY. CODE ALL THAT APPLY.

Children under 5
0 -------------- 0
1 -------------- 1
2 -------------- 2 (50)
3 or more ------ 3

(51)

Children 5 - 14
0 -------------- 0
1 -------------- 1
2 -------------- 2 (51)
3 or more ------ 3

(52)

Q84a Respondent is:

Male --------------------------- 1 (52)
Female ------------------------- 2

Q84b What was your age last birthday?

(53)(54)
99 = refused   [|]   (53/ 54)

(55)

Q85 Is this house/flat owned or rented?

Owned/being bought ----------------- 1 (55)
Rented ----------------------------- 2
Other ------------------------------ 3

139

Q86 Is there a car or van which is normally available for private use by your or a member of your household?

(56)

Yes ----------------------------- 1 (56)
No ------------------------------ 2

Q87a Not counting work, on how many evenings did you go out last week?

0 GO TO Q88a
1 2 3 4 5 6 7 ASK Q87b (57)

Q87b The last time you went out in the evening, how long did you go out for?

(58)

Less than 2 hours ----------------- 1
2 and less than 3 hours ----------- 2
3 and less than 4 hours ----------- 3 (58)
4 and less than 5 hours ----------- 4
5 hours or more ------------------- 5

Q88a Apart from work or shopping for food how much time did you spend out of the house last Saturday?

Q88b And how much time did you spend out of the house last Sunday?

	Q88a	Q88b
	(59)	(60)
Less than 2 hours	1	1
2 and less than 3 hours	2	2
3 and less than 4 hours	3	3
4 and less than 5 hours	4	4
5 hours or more	5	5
None	6	6

(59/60)

Q89 Would you like to go out for pleasure more often?

(61)

Yes ---------------- 1 ASK Q90 (61)
No ----------------- 2 GO TO Q91

Q90 Is there any particular reason why you don't go out more often?

(62)

No-one to go out with ------ 1
Lack of money -------------- 2
Nothing to do -------------- 3 (62)
Too difficult to organise --- 4
Don't have the time -------- 5
Other (WRITE IN)

_____

_____ 6

No particular reason -------- 7

ASK ALL

Q91 Would you like to spend more time with the people who live in your household, or do you spend enough time with them?

(63)

Like to spend more ---------- 1
Enough ---------------------- 2 (63)
Does not apply -------------- 3
Don't know ------------------ 4

140

Q92 SHOWCARD Y How strongly do you agree or disagree with these statements?

		Agree strongly	Agree	Neither	Disagree	Disagree strongly	Don't know	Does not apply
a)	It is more important to spend time with my family than to get on in the world	1	2	3	4	5	6	7 (64)
b)	Everyone needs to get away from their family occasionally	1	2	3	4	5	6	7 (65)
c)	I am happiest when I am with my family	1	2	3	4	5	6	7 (66)
d)	I think about my family a lot when I'm not with them	1	2	3	4	5	6	7 (67)

(68)

Q93 How old were you when you finished your full-time education?

16 or under ------------ 1 GO TO
17 or 18 ---------------- 2 Q95   (68)
19 or over ------------- 3 ASK
Still in full-time   Q94
   education ------------ 4

Q94 What subjects did you specialise in? (FURTHER EDUCATION ONLY)   .   (69)
                                                                              1 2 3 4
_____   5 6 7 8
                                                                              9 0 X Y
_____

                                                            NOW GO TO Q96

Q95 Which subjects did you prefer at school?   (70)
                                                                              1 2 3 4
_____   5 6 7 8
                                                                              9 0 X Y
_____

Q96 SHOWCARD Z Which of these best describes your current position?

                                                            (71)
        Working full-time -------------------------- 1   (71)
        Working part-time -------------------------- 2 ASK Q97a
        Unemployed and looking for work ------------ 3
        Retired ------------------------------------ 4
        Looking after home and family -------------- 5
        Full-time student -------------------------- 6
        Other (WRITE IN)
                                                       7 GO TO Q99
        _____

        ASK Q97 ABOUT RESPONDENT'S PRESENT OR LAST MAIN JOB

Q97a Could you tell me what is/was your job called?

_____

_____

Q97b And what does/did your work actually involve?

_____

_____

141

                                                                              (72)
Q97c Are/were you an employee or self-employed?   Employee -------------- X GO TO e
                                                  Self-employed --------- Y ASK d
                                                                                      BOTH
Q97d Do/did you employ any other people?   None ------------------- 0   IN
     How many?   1 --------------------- 1 NOW   COL
                                                  2 - 24 ---------------- 2 GO TO   72
                                                  25 or more ------------ 3 g

Q97e How many people in total work at the   1 ---------------------- 1
     place where you work/worked?   2 - 24 ---------------- 2   (73)
                                                  25+ ------------------- 3
                                                  Does not apply -------- 4
                                                                 (74)
Q97f Do/did you supervise the work of any   None ------------------- 1   BOTH
     other people? How many?   1 ---------------------- 2   IN
                                                  2 - 24 ---------------- 3   COL
                                                  25+ ------------------- 4   74

Q97g Do/did you regularly do shift work?   Yes -------------------- X
                                                  No --------------------- Y

     IF WORKING ASK Q98. OTHERS GO TO Q99

Q98 SHOWCARD AA I am going to read out a list of statements about work, and for
     each one I would like you to tell me how strongly you agree or disagree
     with it?

                              Agree   Disagree Don't
                              strongly Agree Neither Disagree strongly know

a) My work is very
    monotonous --------------- 1 ----- 2 ----- 3 ------- 4 ------- 5 ----- 6

b) I enjoy having a lot of
    pressure to deal with
    in my work --------------- 7 ----- 8 ----- 9 ------- 0 ------- X ----- Y   (75)

c) If I had a choice I would
    do a different sort of
    job ---------------------- 1 ----- 2 ----- 3 ------- 4 ------- 5 ----- 6

d) I often find myself longing
    for the weekend ---------- 7 ----- 8 ----- 9 ------- 0 ------- X ----- Y   (76)

e) The thing I like about my
    job is that it is team-
    work --------------------- 1 ----- 2 ----- 3 ------- 4 ------- 5 ----- 6

f) My work is interesting
    and satisfying ----------- 7 ----- 8 ----- 9 ------- 0 ------- X ----- Y   (77)

g) I day dream a lot at work -- 1 ----- 2 ----- 3 ------- 4 ------- 5 ----- 6   (78)
    ASK ALL

Q99 The British Film Institute would like to recontact some people in connection
     with this study. Would you mind if we gave your questionnaire to the
     British Film Institute so that, if they want to, they may contact you at
     a later date?
                                                      (79)
                             Yes, willing for questionnaire to
                                be given -------------------------- 1   (79)
                             No, not willing for questionnaire
                                to be given ---------------------- 2

     INTERVIEWER NAME: _____

     INTERVIEWER NUMBER: _____

                                    142

Bibliography

Abrams, M., 'The British Cinema Audience', *Hollywood Quarterly*, 3(2), 1947.

Abrams, M., 'The British Cinema Audience 1949', *Quarterly of Film, Radio and Television*, 4(3), Spring 1950.

Adler, K. P., 'Art Films and Eggheads', *Studies in Public Communication*, Summer 1959.

Adoni, H., 'The Function of Mass Media in the Political Socialisation of Adolescents', *Communication Research* 6, January 1979.

Althede, D. L., 'The Mass Media and Youth Culture', *Urban Education*, 14(2), 1979.

Anast, P., 'Personality Determinants of Mass Media Preferences', *Journalism Quarterly* 43, Winter 1966.

Andrae, T., 'The Culture Industry Reconsidered: Adorno and Mass Culture', *Jump-Cut* 20, 1979.

Augedal, E., 'Patterns in Mass Media Usage and Other Activities', *Acta Sociologica* 15, 1972.

Augst, B., 'The Lure of Psychoanalysis in Film Theory'. In T. H. Kyung Cha (ed.), *The Apparatus*, New York, Tantam Press, 1981.

Austin, B. A., 'Film Attendance: Why college students chose to see their most recent film', *Journal of Popular Film and TV*, 9, Spring 1981.

Austin, B. A., 'Portrait of a Cult Film Audience: *The Rocky Horror Picture Show*', *Journal of Communication*, Spring 1981.

Austin, B. A., 'A Factor Analytic Study of Attitudes Towards Motion Pictures', *Journal of Social Psychology* 117, August 1982.

Austin, B. A., *The Film Audience: An International Bibliography of Research with Annotations and an Essay*, New Jersey, Scarecrow Press, 1983.

Avery, R. K., 'Adolescents' Use of Mass Media', *American Behavioural Scientist* 23, 1979.

Barthes, R., *The Pleasure of the Text*, New York, Hill and Wang, 1974.

Barthes, R., *S/Z*, New York, Hill and Wang, 1975.

Barthes, R., 'Upon Leaving a Movie Theatre.' In T. H. Kyung-Cha (ed.), *The Apparatus.*

Bell, P., 'Identification in a film of Social Control – Siegel and *Dirty Harry*', *Australian Journal of Film Theory* 5/6, 1980.

Belson, W. A., 'The Effects of TV on Movie Going', *Audio-Visual Communication Review* 6, 1958.

Berger, C., 'Viewing as Action: Film and Reader Response Criticism', *Literature and Film* vi, 2, 1978.

Blanchard, S., 'Cinema-Going, Going Gone?' *Screen* vol. 24 nos. 4–5, October 1983.

Blumler, J. G., 'Looking at Media Abundance', *Communications* 5(2–3), 1979.

Board of Trade Journal, 'Effect of Independent Television on Cinema Admissions', 4th August 1956.

Bourdieu, P., 'The Aristocracy of Culture', *Media, Culture and Society* 2, 1980.

Bourdieu, P., *Distinction*, London, Routledge and Kegan Paul, 1985.

Branigan, E., 'The Spectator and Film Space: Two Theories', *Screen* vol. 19 no. 1, 1978.

Britt, S. H., 'What is the Nature of the Drive-In Theatre Audience?' *Media/Scope* June 1960.

Browning, H. E. and Sorrell, A. A., 'Cinemas and Cinema-Going in Great Britain', *Journal of the Royal Statistical Society* Part 11 1954.

Burzynski, M. H. and Dewey, J. B., 'Effect of Positive and Negative Prior Information on Motion Picture Appreciation', *Journal of Social Psychology* 101, April 1977.

Cantwell, J. J., 'The Motion Picture Industry'. In W. J. Perlman (ed.), *The Movies on Trial*, New York, Macmillan, 1936.

Carlson, H. C., 'Movies and the Teenager', *Journal of the Screen Producers Guild* March 1963.

Casetti, F., 'Looking for the Spectator', *Iris* January 1985.

Centre National de la Cinématographie, *Informations*, Bilan 1986, supplément au no. 213, May-June 1987.

Champlin, C., 'Who's watching?', *Journal of The Producers Guild of America*, 15th March 1973.

Coffin, T. E., 'Television's Effect on Leisure-Time Activities', *Journal of Applied Psychology* 32, October 1948.

Collins, W., and Scott, R., 'Mediabank: Cinema', *Marketing Week* 1 February 1985.

Corrigan, P., 'Film Entertainment as Ideology and Pleasure: A Preliminary Approach to a History of the Audience'. In J. Curran and V. Porter (eds.), *Perspectives on British Cinema History*, London, Weidenfeld and Nicolson, 1983.

Cressey, J. G., 'The Motion Picture Experience as Modified by Social Background and Personality', *American Sociological Review* 3 1938.

Daily Mail 11.7.1950, 'Prices, Bad Films Keep People out of the Cinema'.

Dauenhaur, B., 'Authors, Audiences and Texts', *Human Studies* 5(2), 1982.

Dembo, R., 'Gratifications found in Media by British Teenage Boys', *Journalism Quarterly* 5, Autumn 1973.

Dodman, N. D., 'The Cinema Attendance of Adolescents', Paper read to Section J, British Association Meeting, Brighton 1948.

Doscher, L., 'The Significance of Audience Measurement in Motion Pictures', *Journal of Social Issues* 3, Summer 1947.

Douglas, M. and Isherwood, B., *The World of Goods: Toward an Anthropology of Consumption*, London, Allen Lane, 1979.

Douglas, M., and Wollaeger, K., 'Towards a Typology of the Viewing Public'. In Hoggart, R., and Morgan, J. (eds.), *The Future of Broadcasting*, London, Macmillan, 1982.

Downton Advertising, Report on cinema advertising campaign 1985. Unpublished.

Dyer, R., *Stars*. London, British Film Institute, 1982.

Eckert, C., 'The English Cine-Structuralists', *Film Comment* vol. 9 no. 3, May/June 1973.

Elliott, W. R., and Schenk-Hamling, W. J., 'Film, Politics and the Press: The Influence of *All the President's Men*', *Journalism Quarterly* 56, August 1979.

Elliot, B., 'Cities in the Eighties: The Growth of Inequality in UK Society'. In P. Abrams and R. Brown (eds.), *Work, Urbanism and Inequality*, (2nd ed.), London, Weidenfeld and Nicolson, 1984.

Ellis, J., 'Watching Death at Work – an analysis of *A Matter of Life and Death*'. In Ian Christie (ed.), *Powell, Pressburger and Others*, London, British Film Institute, 1978.

England, L., 'What the Cinema means to the British Public'. In R. Manvell (ed.), *The Year's Work in the Film 1949*, London, Longman for the British Council, 1950.

Escarpit, R., 'The Concept of Mass', *Journal of Communication*, 27, 1977.

Ferland, Y., and Voitkus, A., 'Cinema Attendence Habits in Canada', *Canadian Statistical Review* 53, May 1978.

Gaer, F. D., 'The Soviet Film Audience', *Problems of Communication* 23, January 1974.

Gallup Survey 1948 reported in *News Chronicle* 6.4.1948/5.8.1948.

Gans, H. J., '*Star Wars*: The Teenager as Democracy's Saviour', *Social Policy* 8(4), 1978.

Gans, H. J., *Popular Culture and High Culture*, New York, Basic Books, 1975.

Garnham, N., and Williams, R., 'Pierre Bourdieu and the Sociology of Culture: An Introduction', *Media, Culture and Society* 2, 1980.

Garrison, Lee. C, 'The Needs of Motion Picture Audiences', *Californian Management Review* 15, Winter 1972.

Gershuny, J. I. and Thomas, G. S., 'Changing Patterns of Time Use: UK Activity Patterns in 1961 and 1975', Falmer: University of Sussex, Science Policy Research Unit.

Gerson, J., and Boxall, S., 'Opening the Box Office', BFI Internal Document, February 1987.

Gillette, D. C., 'Movies Defy Polls and Projections', *Boxoffice* 108, November 1975.

Glasser, R., *Leisure: Penalty or Prize*, London, Macmillan, 1970.

Goldberg, H. D., 'The Role of Cutting in the Perception of the Motion Picture', *Journal of Applied Psychology* 35, February, 1951.

Gomery, D., 'The Coming of Motion Pictures and the 'Lost' Motion Picture Audience' *Journal of Film and Video*, xxxviii, Summer 1985.

Gray, B., 'The Social Effects of the Film On Children', *Sociological Review*, 42(7), 1950.

Greenberg, H. R., *The Movies on Your Mind*, New York, Basic Books, 1976.

Gregorio, D. D., 'Cinema and TV Audiences in Italy', *Gazette* 11(1), 1965.

Gundlach, R. H., 'The Movies: Stereotypes or Realities', *Journal of Social Issues* 3, Summer 1947.

Hall, J., 'Who goes to the Cinema?', *New Society*, 25 November 1976.

Handel, L., *Hollywood Looks at its Audience*, Urbana, University of Illinois Press, 1950.

Hargreaves, J., 'The Political Economy of Mass Sport'. In S. Parker (et al.), *Sport and Leisure in Contemporary Society*, London: School of Environment, Polytechnic of Central London, 1975.

Hershery, L., 'What Women Think of the Movies', *McCall's* 94, May 1967.

Hoggart, R., *The Uses of Literacy*, London, Chatto and Windus, 1957.

Houston, P., 'Box Office', *Sight and Sound* 44, Winter 1974–5.

Hughes, A. G., *London Children and the Cinema*, London City Council, 1951.

Hulton Reports on Leisure, 1946–55, Hulton Publications.

Jarvie, I. C., *Movies and Society*, New York, Basic Books, 1970.

Jarvie, I. C., 'The Social Experience of Movies'. In S. Thomas, *Film/Culture*, New Jersey, Scarecrow Press, 1982.

Jowett, G. S., 'The First Motion Picture Audience', *Journal of Popular Film*, 3, Winter 1974.

Katz, E. and Lazarsfeld, P., *Personal Influence*, Illinois, Free Press, 1955.

Keir, G., 'Children and the Cinema', *British Journal of Delinquency*, 1(3), 1951.

Kelly, W. P., 'Saturday Night Fever', *Journal of American Culture* 2(2), Summer 1979.

Kinematograph Weekly, 'New Survey Probes Film Going Habits', 6 November 1958.

Kinematograph Weekly, 'Cinema-Going in London', May 14/21/28, June 4/11/18 1964.

Kippax, S. and Murray, J. P., 'Using the Mass Media: Need Gratification and Perceived Utility', *Communication Research* 7, July 1980.

Kracauer, S., *Theory of Film*, Oxford, Oxford University Press, 1960.

Lawless, P. and Brown, F., *Urban Growth and Change in Britain*, London, Harper and Row, 1986.

Leeks, R. A., 'Colour and the Box Office', *British Kinematography* vol. 35(6), December 1959.

Lewis, G. H., 'Taste Cultures and their Compositions: Toward a New Theoretical Perspective'. In Katz, E. and Szescko, T. (eds.), *Mass Media and Social Change*, Sage, Beverly Hills and London, 1980.

Lewis, G. H., 'The Differentiation of Popular Culture Audiences', *Journal of Popular Culture* 11, Fall 1977.

Licher, P. S., 'Code and Code Shifting in Film Communication'. *Semiotica*, 39(3–4), 1982.

Linton, J., 'But it's only a Movie'. *Jump Cut* 17, 1978.

Livant, B., 'The Audience Commodity', *Canadian Journal of Social and Political Theory* 3(1), 1979.

Lassner, R., 'Sex and Age Determinants of Theatre and Movie Interests', *Journal of General Psychology* 31, October 1944.

Lorimor, E. S. and Dunn, S. W., 'Use of Mass Media in France and Egypt', *Public Opinion Quarterly* 32, Winter 1968–9.

Low, R., 'The Implications behind the Social Survey'. In R. Manvell (ed.), *The Penguin Film Review* no. 2. London, Penguin, 1949.

Lyness, P. I., 'Patterns in the Mass Communications Tastes of Young People', *Journal of Educational Psychology*, December 1951.

Mayer, J. P., *British Cinemas and their Audience: Sociological Studies*, London, Dobson, 1948.

Mayer, J. P., *Sociology of Film, Studies and Documents*, London, Faber and Faber, 1946.

Metz, C., 'The Imaginary Signifier', *Screen*, vol. 16 no. 2, 1975.

Morley, D., *The Nationwide Audience*, London, British Film Institute, 1980.

Moss, L. and Box, K., *The Cinema Audience*. An Inquiry made by the Wartime Social Survey for the Ministry of Information, London, Ministry of Information Social Survey Report, New Series, 37b 1943.

Munsterberg, H., *The Photoplay: A Psychological Study*, New York, Dover, 1970.

National Council of Public Morals, Cinema Commission of Inquiry, *The*

Cinema, its Present Position and Future Possibilities; Report and Evidence taken by the Cinema Commission of Inquiry instituted by the National Council of Public Morals, London, Williams and Norgate, 1917.

Parker, S., 'Leisure'. In R. G. Burgess (ed.), *Key Variables in Social Investigation*, London, Routledge and Kegan Paul, 1986.

Parker, S., *The Sociology of Leisure*, London, Allen and Unwin, 1976.

Perlman, W. J. (ed.), *The Movies on Trial*, New York, Macmillan, 1936.

Political and Economic Planning Office, *The British Film Industry* 1952 and 1958, PEP, 1952, 1958.

Powell, D., 'The Development of the Film in Educational and Social Life', *Journal of the Royal Society of Arts*, 14 January 1949.

Roberts, K., *Youth and Leisure*, London, George Allen and Unwin, 1983.

Robinson, D. C., 'Television/Film Attitudes of Upper-Middle Class Professionals', *Journal of Broadcasting* 19(2), Spring 1975.

Roddick, N., 'New Audiences, New Films'. In M. Auty and N. Roddick (eds.), *British Cinema Now*, London, British Film Institute, 1985.

Rojek, C., *Capitalism and Leisure Theory*, London, Tavistock, 1985.

Rosenberg, B. and White, D. M., *Mass Culture*, Illinois, Free Press, 1957.

Sherman, B., *Working at Leisure*, London, Methuen, 1986.

Silvery, R. and Kenyon, J., 'Why You Go to the Pictures, a BBC report', *Films and Filming*, June 1965.

Simon, A. A., 'Quantitative, Nonreactive Study of Mass Behaviour with Emphasis on the Cinema', *Psychological Reports* 48(3), 1981.

Spraos, J., *The Economic Decline of the Cinema*, London, George Allen and Unwin, 1962.

Thomas, S., (ed.), *Film/Culture: Explorations of the Cinema in its Social Context*, New Jersey, Scarecrow Press, 1982.

Thurston, L. L., 'A Scale for Measuring Attitude Towards The Movies', *Journal of Educational Research* 22, 1930.

McFarling, T., 'UK Cinema Audience Increase Confirmed', *Screen International*, 1 February 1986.

Tudor, A., *Image and Influence*, London, George Allen and Unwin, 1975.

US Information Agency (see) 'American Films and Foreign Audiences', *Film Comment* 3, 1965.

Vargas, A. L., 'British Films and their Audience', In R. Manvell (ed.), *The Penguin Film Review*, no 8, London, Penguin, 1949.

Wall, W. D. and Simson, W., 'The Effects of Cinema Attendance on the Behaviour of Adolescents as seen by their Contemporaries', *British Journal of Educational Psychology*, February, 1949.

Ward, J. C., *Children and the Cinema: an Inquiry made by the Social Survey in October 1948 for a Department Committee...*, London, Central Office of Information, 1949; Social Survey Report, New Series, no. 131.

Wilkinson, F., 'The Cinema as a Social Force', *Visual Education*, October 1958.

Williams, R., *Communications*, London, Pelican, 1962.

Young, K., 'Review of the Payne Foundation Studies', *American Journal of Sociology*, September 1935.

Young, M. and Wilmott, P., *Family and Kinship in East London*, London, Penguin, 1969.

Young, M. and Wilmott, P., *The Symmetrical Family*, London, Penguin, 1975.

Index